STEPPING STONES TO BETHLEHEM

With love and sincere gratitude to
Carol Ann, Brian, Shane, Kevin, and Fiona,
who generously provided me with the
perfect setting, and ideal conditions,
(and the computer!)
in which
I have been able to write this book.

JACK McARDLE SS CC

Stepping Stones to Bethlehem

DAILY REFLECTIONS FOR ADVENT

THE COLUMBA PRESS
DUBLIN 2003

THE COLUMBA PRESS
55A Spruce Avenue, Stillorgan Industrial Park,
Blackrock, Co Dublin

First edition 2002
Cover by Bill Bolger
Origination by
The Columba Press
Printed in Ireland by
ColourBooks Ltd, Dublin

ISBN 1 85607 422 6

CONTENTS

Introduction

There are many books on the market that help us make the most of Advent, and to prepare for Christmas as best we can. I make no pretence that this present offering is any better, or any more original than those already available. All I can claim for it is that it is a collection of some of my own thoughts, reflections, decisions, and whispered prayers during the weeks of Advent.

By the nature of things there will, of course, be repetition. I couldn't hope, or wouldn't attempt to write reflections for every day of Advent without words like redemption, gift, invitation, response, and, above all, *love*, being mentioned on nearly every page. I am only too aware that, in our everyday world, each of us takes responsibility for our own preparations for Christmas. After all, in that everyday world, we have to do our own shopping, buy our own gifts, and – worst of all for me! – put up the decorations, and set up the Christmas tree! It is precisely because of the pressures of all these chores that this book is prepared and presented. If I am too busy to pray, then I'm too busy. It would be sad, at the very least, if a Christian approached Christmas as a time for shopping, decorating, and providing, without specific reference to what the season is all about. By all means, let us celebrate, give and receive gifts, and enjoy ourselves to our heart's content. However, at the risk of repetition, as a Christian, I must be faced with priorities, and I must strive to get those priorities right.

This book presents a reflection for each day. The titles are chosen at random, and I gave no great thought to importance or sequence. There are a few thoughts presented for consideration and reflection. These are quite short, because, as I mentioned above, there can be so many demands on one's time, that anything longer might be beyond the scope of one's available time. I don't claim anything profound or original in these reflections, beyond hoping that a sentence here or there might stir up further reflection when the booklet has been laid aside.

The second part contains a suggestion or two about something that might get my particular attention on that day. I deliberately avoided being too specific in these, because I trust the goodwill of the reader to take the suggestions offered, and to mediate them down into the specific. To do so is the test of our sincerity. We all can be very good at generalities and, if sincerity is absent, we tend to remain at that stage.

The final part of each day's offering is a short prayer. Once again, this is just intended as a kick-off point, from which further prayers and expressions of the same disposition might possibly come into the heart at a later time in the day. The words are not important; rather it is the intent contained in the words. Some of our 'better' prayers quite often don't require words.

I have enjoyed writing these reflections. I strongly believe that a life without reflection is a life that's not worth living. I cannot do another's reflecting for him or her, but my hope is that these thoughts might serve as a catalyst, as a kind of jump-start, and that some of what is read in the morning might resurface from time to time during the day. Naturally, it is my hope that each reflection might be read first thing in the morning, whenever possible. It would make little sense to me to read a reflection, for the first time, last thing at night, unless some readers discover that my writing helps put them to sleep! I present this booklet with my love, and my sincere wishes that it provides the reader with at least some of the many blessings that I have prayed for in the writing.

FIRST SUNDAY OF ADVENT

Waken up!

We are familiar with the experience of a foot or a hand 'going to sleep', or having that tingling sensation that forces us to wait a while, until the sensation is gone, before attempting to put pressure on the foot, or lift something with the hand. This is often called 'pins and needles', because of the sensation we experience. We know this will pass and, personally, I have never tried to analyse what is causing this. We just know that it will go away, and that both limbs will be up and running within less than a minute. We experience other occasions when some part of the body is not fully alert, especially if I am not a 'morning person'. Some people get out of bed at 8.00am, and the body is not yet fully alert and awake for an hour or two later! I myself happen to be a 'morning person', and I'm sure there have been times when a member of my community has had to restrain the annoyance experienced towards me, if the other is still half-asleep, even if washed, dressed, and seemingly functioning normally.

Each new morning is a unique and special gift, never before given to a person, and never again available to anybody. Because it is a gift, it may be appropriately called the 'present'. Written on the gift are the words 'Batteries included'. With the day comes all that is needed to live this day to the full, within the limits of my physical or mental abilities. We pass through levels of awareness, however, before we become fully aware of the gift that is given, and of the time that is passing. We can drift, rather than step out; exist rather than live. Everybody dies, but not everybody lives. I have a much greater concern about living life to the full while I am still alive, than any concerns I may have about life after death. When today becomes exactly like yesterday, then I may have lost the plot. Alice in Wonderland begins her story with the words, 'I could tell you my story beginning this morning. I couldn't begin yesterday, because I was a different person then.' Cardinal Suenens said that his God was new with each new day. Today is yet another 'Yes' from God to me; and I cannot live today on a 'yes' I said yesterday.

Advent is a wake-up call. 'Arise from your slumbers …' Jesus tells the story of those who were distracted, and totally unprepared when the bridegroom returned from the feast (Mt 25:10). For the Jews, the Messiah had been promised, and was long awaited. When Jesus came, however, they were caught napping. God never comes at the right time! Jesus says, 'You know not the day nor the hour when the Son of Man will come' (Mt 24:42). Advent is a time of intensive alertness and preparation, because, in our day, we know that the Lord will come to any of us when we are ready to receive him. His coming is not confined to Christmas, or to the day of Judgement. We speak of the First Coming, and the Final Coming, but Jesus is more than willing to come to us every moment of every day and, if we allow him, make his home in our hearts. There is no reason that he should ever leave us. For our purposes, during this Advent Season, we will concentrate on Christmas as a time when we will be ready, willing, and longing to welcome him.

Action

Whenever you can today, pause for a few moments. Gather your thoughts, check on the time, and become aware of your surroundings. Become as *present* in that moment, in that place, with those people, as you possibly can. See how many times, today, you can actually pull yourself together, come into the *present moment*, and become aware of that. Think of this as 'checking in', just to ensure that you are alert, awake, and aware. That would be a good first step on the road to Bethlehem ...

Prayer

Mary, my Mother, caretaker of my heart, please help me to be alert and to be conscious of the gift of this day. Accompany me today, and like a mother and her child, waken me up when you think I should be awake!

FIRST MONDAY OF ADVENT

Listening

One way of 'wakening up' is to become a good listener. I need to learn to listen, before I begin to listen to learn. I myself find that I am not good at remembering names. When I examine this, I discover that I had not given much attention when I was introduced to someone by name. The name went over my head, or in one ear and out the other. What was missing was a genuine attentive interest, and there was some part of my brain not switched on when the name was mentioned. At some time or another, all of us have found ourselves speaking to someone, and, after a pause, the person turns to us with 'Sorry. What did you say?' The lights were on, but there was nobody at home. Being a good listener is a wonderful gift, because creative listening generates creative sharing. Like a computer, the proper 'mode' button may not be switched to 'on'.

During a time like Advent, I can easily convince myself that 'I have heard it all before' but, in reality, I know rightly that this is not true. I can hear something new every time I listen to a passage of scripture, depending on whether I'm listening with my ears, or with my heart. When I listen with the heart, the message is always new and refreshing. I have heard it said that I have two ears and one tongue, so I should listen twice as much as I speak. I have also heard the advice to take the cotton wool out of one's ears, and put it in the mouth instead! It would prove to be an excellent way of opening my heart to the message of Advent, by paying particular attention to how I really listen to others. This, of course, also applies to prayer, which can often be more about God speaking to me, rather than me speaking to God. There's a big difference between 'Speak, Lord, your servant is listening', and 'Listen, Lord, your servant is speaking'!

I grew up in the country before the advent of radio, TV, computers, or mobile phones. We had what we called a wireless, which, without the luxury of electricity, was run on batteries. We had one station, and that was our everyday contact with the big wide world out there. One of the more frequent problems we had was that it had what I might call a 'drifting dial', which meant that it required regular adjustment to bring it back on the station. I cannot remember thinking of this as a major problem, because we accepted it just as part of the way the thing worked. I often think of that situation today, when it comes to listening. In one way or another, we all can have a drifting dial, and we need to turn our hearing back on the wavelength again. Not giving others our full attention, as they speak, can often be insensitive, if not downright rude. As part of the awakening process that goes into our Advent preparation, it would help greatly if we gave more attention to how we listen, whether that is to others, to the Word of God, or to the Lord himself. I cannot hope, in these short reflections, to examine all the different ways in which parts of our being can be quite dormant, but I hope to deal with some of them during this first week.

Action

I would suggest that, for today, I decide to take a regular 'rain-check' on my listening. I make a decision this morning that I will deliberately tune up my listening, and make every effort I can to give my full attention to what others are saying to me, or to what is read at Mass, and even to what my inner spirit is saying. There is always a voice speaking to me, whether that be another person, an inspiration of the Spirit, or the still inner voice of my own conscience. I want to develop a proper frame of mind during this time of preparation, and to upgrade my level of listening would be one excellent way to do this. It would be a very worthwhile exercise if I readjusted my drifting dial from time to time today.

Prayer

Spirit of God, please draw my attention today to what is being said, and to how I am listening. Please give me a listening heart. Through your presence and action within me, make me more and more alert to what is going on around me and, especially to what others are saying to me.

FIRST TUESDAY OF ADVENT

Speaking

The gift of speech is something that God gives me for others. He doesn't give me my gift of speech to go around talking to myself! It is said that I should never put my mouth in motion until my brain is in gear! Words can sometimes be the weakest form of communication. Words, in themselves, can be lifeless. Someone may ask me how I am, and I hesitate to answer, because I'm not convinced that he/she really wants to know! Someone else may ask the very same question, using exactly the same words, and I sit down and tell them – sometimes to an extent that they're sorry they asked me! It is the spirit in the words that gives them life. I could call you all kinds of names today, and you might react with hilarious laughter, because you know that I'm only joking. On another occasion I could call you the very same names, and you are deeply hurt, because you know that, today, I mean what I say.

As we prepare for Christmas, I need to remind myself about the many ways we wish others the joys and blessings of the season. Once again, these can be sincere, or meaningless. Christmas is a time for gift-giving, and it would be good to remember that speech is a very precious gift in itself, and can be a very powerful gift to others. To avoid speech being mere words that are spoken with the tongue, with no depth or sincerity in them, it would be wonderful if we considered the heart as the organ God gave us with which to speak. If I speak from the heart, I speak to the heart. When we come closer to Christmas, I will be reflecting a great deal on the heart as our Bethlehem today. When I reflect on immediate preparations, I will be speaking about ridding the stable, the manger of our hearts, so that Jesus will be really welcomed there. As this stage, I am suggesting, by way of remote preparation, that I reflect on the heart as the source of my sharing, including the words I say, and the things I do.

The Holy Spirit plays a very central role in all of this. Jesus speaks of the Spirit as a Spirit of Truth. Truth, sincerity, genuineness, warmth, etc., are all beautiful qualities in my use of the gift of speech. Speaking can actually be a very real Christian ministry, and I'm not referring to preaching here. I am referring to sincere sharing, to confirming others through my words, and especially to paying particular attention to the words I use when I pray. Of course, I don't need to use words when I pray, but in a lot of our praying, such as liturgies, rosaries, novenas, or chaplets, we can so easily slip into a routine of rattling off words, where we honour God with our lips while our hearts are far from him. I'm sure it never happened, but I did hear about a bishop who dreamt he was preaching a sermon and, when he woke up, he discovered he was! Words can be very life-giving when the speaker puts life into them. During our Advent liturgies, it would be helpful if I were aware that the readings are God speaking to me. It would be very enriching indeed, in my preparation for Christmas, if I had an openness to what God is saying to all of us. His final Word will be spoken on Christmas day.

ACTION

Try to concentrate today to ensure that your words are coming from your heart. Use your words to confirm and build up others. Avoid criticism, exaggeration, and boasting. Try to make the listener feel important enough by the warmth and sincerity of your speech. Choose kind words, and avoid words that can give offence. At the end of the day, it would be good to try to identify occasions when my words were spoken with sincerity, in a way that really helped the listener.

PRAYER

Spirit of God, Spirit of Truth, please be in every word I speak today. May you touch the hearts of others through my words. Please help me make full use of this wonderful gift for the benefit of others, and raise my consciousness of the possibility for good that my words can contain.

FIRST WEDNESDAY OF ADVENT

Reflecting

Continuing on our 'wake-up' journey this week, it might be good to go down into our own hearts today, and check out how much life we find there. A life without reflection is not worth living. It is so easy to slip into some level of superficial living, where I skim off the surface, without depth or dedication. I often wonder what must happen to a person who is working on a conveyer belt, whose job might be something like this: Microchips are moving one after another along the conveyer belt. The worker stands there with a soldering iron and, as each chip passes, he tips one spot on it, and sends it in on its way. Imagine doing this day after day, after day, after day ... Not must scope for individual initiative here. Hard to imagine any great personal stimulation. Today becomes like yesterday, and he knows what he'll be doing this time next week. I know this may be a reality for some people but, thankfully, not for most. I use this example to show how the inner me can become completely detached from what the outer me is doing. I become a robot and, apart from my hands and eyes, there is none of me engaged in what I'm doing.

Imagine, if you will, that the conveyer belt stops, and I invite the worker to come aside for a while. I invite him/her to stretch out for a bit, to relax, and to 'flop' on a beanbag. Relax, relax, relax ...; this is *Time out!* Forget about the solder, the chips, and the conveyer belt. 'This is *your* time!' Let the muddy water settle inside, as you go down into the heart, and become aware of what's happening there. Here is a chance for you to get in touch with *you*. As you enter your heart, you discover yet another conveyer belt! The difference now, however, is that you don't have to do anything! This conveyer belt is carrying feelings, emotions, insights, and thoughts. Once again, you don't have to do anything. Just observe, get in touch, become aware of what is happening within. Zen Buddists speak of the inner pearl of great price. This pearl rests at the very core of our being. Unfortunately, however, it is a pearl in muddy water. It is only when we relax, become still, and settle down within, that the muddy water settles, and the pearl becomes visible. Part of my preparation for Christmas must make me more and more aware of the manger of my heart. If I am to prepare my heart, I must go down, and enter the heart. Today need involve nothing more than locating the heart, as it were, and becoming more conscious of it. Oh, I know where my heart is, of course, but I'm not speaking of the physical heart here. I use the word 'heart' to speak of that part of me where I am most authentic, where the real me is living. It is where I am most at home, when I take time out to visit. Despite the masks I wear, the games I play, the barriers I erect, there is that authentic self, often unacknowledged, that is found at the core of my being.

This place is like my inner Prayer Room, my own special refuge. It is a place where I can feel safe and, from this safe place, I can look out at life from time to time. It is my 'Time Out' dug-out, my chapel, my Temple, my Mosque. I can go there to pray and to reflect. It is in this very place that Jesus hopes to receive a welcome this Christmas.

Action

Make a point of talking time out today. You will find those moments if your heart is open to doing so. If you are too busy to do this, then you are too busy! Listen to the still quiet voice of that inner self, and hear what it has to say. How are you feeling, … I mean, how are you really feeling? How is today going for you? Take time out to look out at life, for a change. You are so much more than the work you do, the chores you perform, the role you play. Try not to get sucked into activities so much that you become so preoccupied with the urgent that you neglect the important. Make sure that you yourself are not on a conveyer belt, moving from one activity to another, where you will have lost your own self in the process. 'What does it profit a person to gain the whole world, and suffer the loss of one's own soul?'

Prayer

Lord Jesus, I invite you to sit down with me at the table of my heart for a minute or two. What do you need to say to me, Lord? Have you been waiting patiently for me to give you a few minutes of my attention? Please help me to become more aware of your presence, and to turn to you more frequently, even if only for a moment of acknowledging your presence.

FIRST THURSDAY OF ADVENT

Moving Statues?

A few years ago, in Ireland, there was a great stir about statues of Our Lady that were seen to move, in several places throughout the land. These drew widespread attention, both in the media and among the people at large, often resulting in huge crowds flocking to the places where the phenomenon was reported as happening. It is not my place, nor is it within the competence of my expertise, to pass judgment on the authenticity of such events. I mention this here now, because I want to use this to illustrate a point of how things could be within my own life. There are times when I myself can become like a statute, but in this case the statue is not moving! I can get stuck in inactivity, without growth, movement, or human development. I can become like a rabbit caught in the headlights of an oncoming car. 'Petrus' is the Latin word for stone, and I can become 'petrified', becoming like a stone, or a rock, that is motionless, remaining in the one spot for ages. Life is dynamic, it continues to move, whether I am aware of that or not. If I'm not moving forward, I am automatically moving backwards. Relationships are like that. A married couple may be totally unaware that their relationship is moving backwards, until they wake up and discover that they have nothing to say to one another. They never deliberately chose to do so; it just happened, because they were making no effort to move the relationship forward.

Albert Camus, in a novel called *The Fall,* speaks of a

man who took no action, while being aware that he should do something about what was happening around him. Camus writes, 'He did nothing, because that was the kind of man he was.' That is a chilling prase. How often do we hear that all it takes for evil to succeed, is that good people should do nothing? At Christmas-time, we celebrate a most extraordinary action by God. God took the initiative in doing something to redeem the world, and bring his people back to the Garden. We read about the three wise men who travelled a long distance to investigate a sign they had read in the heavens. The shepherds were given a message by angels and, at once, they sprang into action, to go and see this for themselves. Over the Christmas time, we visit relatives, friends, or communicate with acquaintances through cards, phone calls, etc. Christmas does call us into action. Witness the shopping throngs in our high streets in the weeks coming up to Christmas, and the whole town seems to be more alive, alert, and on the move than it has been for the previous twelve months.

The action I wish to focus on here has to do with my own personal life. All diets start on Monday, never today! As I prepare for Christmas, I surely must become aware that this is a time for up and doing. When spring comes, we become involved with spring-cleaning, gardening, and painting. Summer includes a variety of activities that are almost exclusive to that time of year, as the children get their buckets and spades, or the parents roll the barbeque out of the garage. For the Christian, Christmas calls for very specific activity, as we prepare our hearts for what we are about to celebrate. During the next few weeks I intend becoming more specific about some of the action that needs to be undertaken. For now, though, I just want to focus on action in general. God's action must generate a response from us, because there's nothing automatic about God. Jesus came 'for the fall as well as for the resurrection of many'. St. Paul tells us that our salvation is based on two things: What Jesus has done for us, and how we respond to that. Communication is at least two-way, or it's no-way. I grew up with the idea that 'resolutions' (those things that would make me a better person) were confined to New Year's Day, Ash Wednesday, or the Annual Retreat or parish Mission. That let me off the hook for all the other days of the year!

Action

Without necessarily getting too specific, at this stage, can you identify some things that must be faced up to in your life, if there is to be any sincerity involved in your preparation for Christmas? Surely, at least, I must acknowledge that this Christmas is not, and cannot be exactly the same as last year. This holds true, no matter how good or special last Christmas may have been. This Christmas is unique; it never happened before, and it will never happen again. It's a once-off, and the graces available this time round are uniquely part of God's special gifts to me at this time. Identifying today some areas calling for action, will prove a great help in the coming days, when we become more specific about what those actions should be. Suffice for now to put down a marker, as a reminder that, no matter how much or how long we reflect on Christmas and its significance, our response must include action of some kind or other. Rather than asking you how you feel about the up-coming season, I am asking you what you intend doing as part of your response to the season that is in it.

Prayer

Mary, my Mother, as you continue preparing the manger of my heart, please draw my attention to areas and items within my heart, and in my life, that I must face up to, and be willing to act on, to make it possible for you to do your work. You didn't stay on in Bethlehem, because there were other things to do, and other places to go. Please take my hand, and lead me to the manger, and then wherever you see fit, let me turn my face and travel on my Christian journey.

FIRST FRIDAY OF ADVENT

A Journey

Prayer is a journey. It is a journey from the head to the heart. It is a journey from the Holy of Holies, where the Pharisee is boasting about his own goodness, to the back, where the Publican is declaring himself a sinner. It is a journey from the good-hearted but 'pre-occupying' actions of Martha, to the quiet listening and contemplation of Mary. To reach Bethlehem, Mary and Joseph had to travel from the north of the country, to a very remote part, a long distance away. Mary had her own personal journey over the previous nine months, from the time the Angel presented her with a message from God, to the time that that message was about to become flesh. It was a time of much prayer, quiet reflection, and growing submission to the will of 'He that is Mighty'. At no time was she is possession of all the facts and possibilities. It was a journey of faith, of humble acceptance of a promise from God that someone with her humble spirit would not ever dare to question. Her prayer was one of humble and expectant waiting. Prayer, whether the psalms of her people, or the pondering in her heart, was her main and greatest preparation for what was to come. I couldn't imagine her saying long prayers! Sometimes 'long prayers' create a situation where God has to shut up and listen, because I am speaking! She would be more of a 'Speak, Lord, your servant is listening' kind of person, when she prayed.

I have come across people of my generation, who,

through no fault of their own, were still living with a First Communion level of spirituality. They had the exact same morning and night prayers that they learned in school; their confessions were a repetition of the good old laundry list, memorised for First Confession, and they continued to read their own prayers from a prayer book, totally detached from what the priest might be saying or doing on the altar. Just imagine, if you will, what would happen if you met the same people every single day, and you repeated the exact same conversation day after day, after day. Something would have to give! You might soon discover that those people don't seem to be around any more, and you're wondering what has happened to them! There is a certain nostalgia about Christmas and I think it's true to say that we all love to welcome the return of 'Silent Night', 'Adeste', etc (except for the small groups of kids at our front doors before the month of December has begun!). Personally, I welcome the traditional crib, the holly, the poinsettia, etc. I would have good reason to be concerned, however, if the level of my sense of involvement, or rather the depth of it, hasn't moved a bit since the previous Christmas. I have just spent another year of gestation within the womb of God, and it is only reasonable to expect some evidence that the formation of Christ within me is becoming a little bit more evident. I would feel uneasy in the presence of someone who was quite happy with the level, scope, and diversity of their prayer-life, because I consider this as something that is always and continuously evolving. In practical terms, if I make a habit of devoting a certain length of time with the Lord each day, I am almost certain that he will be looking for at least twice that amount of time a year later. Moving along this pathway of time spent in prayer is also part of the journey. This is but the first week of Advent, and I am deliberately keeping these reflections quite general, in the hope of becoming more specific as Christmas approaches. All I want to do now is evoke some sort of awakening to ideas and concepts that may have become dormant or stagnant and then, in the next few weeks, to face up to these full on.

Action

Take some time out today to check out your prayer-life, especially as to the prayers themselves, the source of your prayers (book, leaflets, rosaries, spontaneous, etc), and the structures of your prayer-time, relative to frequency, place, and times. Let there be no condemnation whatever involved in this, because it is not an examination of conscience. It is just a brief stock-taking, or rain-check of how things actually are. No need for resolutions at this stage. Please also avoid comparing! Just because X or Y spends two hours in prayer every day, doesn't mean that you should be doing the same. Make this brief check for your sake only and, hopefully, over the next few weeks in these reflections, you will find some ideas and suggestions that may help you, no matter where you're at on the journey. Just hold on to this one point that can never be up for discussion: I must find time for prayer, and this must be serious and sincere enough that I will ensure a definite time and place, whenever possible. I am sure of a few meals a day, and the times and places where I will be for those meals. What I am saying here is that prayer should get at least the same priority, and be given the same importance.

Prayer

Mary, my Mother, please take up residence as the care-taker of my heart, and obtain for me the especial grace of having a praying heart; a heart that would not always need words to communicate with God. From within my heart, let your gentle promptings be my constant reminders to give some time and space to God at particular times. Like a mother ensuring that her child doesn't run off to school without a breakfast, please continue to be a real Mother for me.

FIRST SATURDAY OF ADVENT

Decision Time

There's nothing more powerful than an idea whose time has come. There is no scarcity of ideas! The road to hell is paved with good intentions. I know I run the risk of being repetitive in the reflections for this first week, but I want to stress in every possible way the need for us to waken up, and become totally alert as we approach this beautiful and grace-filled season. Much of what I've shared up till now could easily be catalogued under the heading of 'Nice ideas! I must get around to that some-time!' One of the greatest sermons in the Acts of the Apostles is that given by Paul in Athens, when he came across the statue to the Unknown God. He waxed eloquently about who this Unknown God was, and he proceeded to tell them about Jesus, his message, and need for all of them to respond to that message. He spoke at some length and, one would have thought, to good effect, and at the end of all his efforts, the people remarked to one another, 'That's very interesting; we must hear him again sometime!' Poor Paul! Jesus experienced this kind of response on many an occasion. I myself have read many a book, listened to many a talk, that really impressed me but, alas, with the passage of time, the impression just faded and, to use a phrase that has a certain sadness about it, 'I never just got around to it'. I sometimes wonder what it might feel like to be on one's death-bed, recalling all those wonderful and exciting inspirations that I just never got around to.

I could sound the clarion call of Christmas, and pro-claim 'The time has come!' 'Prepare ye the way of the Lord.' 'Awake from your slumber, arise from your sleep.' However, there is one point in particular that I want to really stress right now. No matter what God made possi-ble for us as a result of that first Christmas night, he will never make our decisions or our choices for us. If Jesus stood in front of a group of people today, as he often did in the past, and spoke his message, he then would go over, sit down on the stump of a tree, and await the response to his word. The response must come from us, and that is why we will be held responsible for the mes-sage we have received. Not to respond is, in itself, a response. 'No' is also an answer to prayer! To make deci-sions is to be decisive, and this leads to achievement and accomplishment. The gospels are not just a collection of nice ideas. Jesus came 'to do and to teach'. He washed his disciples' feet, and then, and only then, did he ask them to do the same. He fed the hungry, and he now asks us to do likewise. The gospels call to action, and decisions that don't lead to action are dead. 'Faith without good works is dead,' scripture tells us. This may seem just a rehashing of the 'Moving Statues' reflection of Thursday last, but I think it's important that, at the risk of repetition, we begin to take control of things, and be up and doing, rather than dreaming dreams, as the sands of time run out.

I remember some years ago, I had occasion to attend a monthly meeting having to do with community living, and apostolates. A few minutes before the end of the meeting, one member would slip out of the room to organise some tea and biscuits before the troops scattered to their various locations. There was a press just behind the door, with a banner rolled up in the top drawer. This banner was very quietly unfurled and hung on the back of the door, to face each of us as we got up to leave. The banner read 'Do it, damn it!' We had spent the previous few hours speaking about wonderful plans, hopes, and expectations, and I always felt that I needed that last kick in the behind, as I left; otherwise I had just wasted some valuable time that brought no result. I couldn't imagine any genuine preparation for Christmas that did not include some serious decision-making. What exactly those decisions might be will be included in other reflections, as we come nearer to Christmas day itself.

Action

How do you rate yourself, in general, in the decision-making stakes? Do you know someone who always seems to have problems making decisions? How do you compare? Make one simple decision this morning; be quite specific about time, action, and your own sincerity in carrying it out. See how you do. It doesn't have to be a difficult decision, but it is better if it is something that you have been postponing, or trying to avoid. I'm sure you know what I mean, and that I'm not thinking of a decision to eat your dinner, or watch television. I find that if there's an important football match on the television, I will remember that, rearrange other plans I may have had, if possible, and I'll be right there in front of the television well before kick-off time! Quite often our track-record in the decision-making area is directly related to the level of our sincerity and our maturity. When the result of the decision involves something that's for my good, the struggle to act is usually much easier – which should tell us something!

Prayer

Spirit and Breath, and Power of God, I ask you, please, to inspire me today, and prompt me into making and carrying out my decisions. Please remind me and, as Spirit of Truth, help me to be faithful to my decisions, and to be true to my promises. I look to you to energise me into action, and to stir up within me a zeal and enthusiasm for things of God. Enkindle within me the fires of divine love, and move from being a gentle breeze to becoming a whirlwind if that's what it takes to get me into action.

SECOND SUNDAY OF ADVENT

The Gospel is Now

One of the problems that could be creating a barrier to my proper reading and understanding of the gospels is that I might read them as I read a history book. These are events and situations that happened all those years ago, and all I'm doing now is remembering them, recalling them, and learning something from them. I know that Jesus was born only once, and that he died only once. However, there is another dimension that must be taken into account. What happened all those years ago has not really happened for me until it actually happens within my heart. Incarnation and redemption is something that is ongoing. The events of then have to happen all over again within the hearts of each one of us. In other words, as far as I am concerned, the gospel is *now*, and I am every person in the gospel. Unlike Mary, I may not see or hear the Angel with my human senses, but God sends that same message to every one of us. 'Do you agree to become God's instrument for making Jesus present in today's world?' Like Mary, I may well ask how can I do this? And once again comes the reply and the reassurance: 'The Holy Spirit will come upon you, and the power of the Most High will overshadow you.' That is how incarnation takes place in each of us today. Jesus is a personal God. 'Who do *you* say that I am? Will *you* also go away? Do *you* love me more than these?'

The Christian community is entrusted with the same vocation as Mary, i.e. to form the Body of Christ, and to make Jesus present in today's world. We differ from Mary in so far as she was alone, and had full responsibility for her answer. As a member of the Christian community, I share this responsibility with other members of the community. This does not take away my own individual and personal freedom, however, because each member of the body has the freedom to accept or reject the offer. Once I respond as a member of the community, I lose my individual freedom, as it were, because community living makes demands, and places responsibilities on my shoulders. Once I become a member of a body, like a foot, I am no longer free to go off for a walk on my own. The foot, of course, can become gangrenous, and may have to be amputated, because it is no longer able to avail of the life-flowing blood of the rest of the body. Judas was free to walk away, and Jesus wouldn't stop him, even though he tried everything to get Judas to reflect on what he was doing.

The point I am making in this reflection is that it can bring everything into much clearer focus if I think of the gospel as something that is unfolding in my own life, and in the life of the Christian community to which I belong. More important than the Christmas tree, the decorations, the pudding, or the turkey, are the preparations I myself make to ensure that Christmas really does happen within my heart. I, too, can have wise men and shepherds of one kind or another crossing my path is search of evidence that Jesus is alive and well, and living among us. My vocation is to be an ambassador for Christ, and to represent him wherever I go. The people I meet may never buy the book, and I may be the only gospel they may ever read. 'You write a new page of the gospels each day through the things that you do, and the words that you say. People read what you write, whether faithful or true. What is the gospel according to you?'

Action

Find some quiet place and some quiet time today, and put yourself in Mary's place, when the Angel appeared to her. You are the one the Lord has chosen through whom he wants to become incarnate today. Hear that promise about the Holy Spirit making it all possible, and give some serious reflection about what your answer is. There are so many others whose lives can be effected for good by your *yes* to that invitation. You have your own personal vocation, and you are offered the privilege of providing the manger of your heart for the great mystery of salvation and redemption to be played out all over again. God invites you to become personally involved in his plan for the world. What a privilege is ours! This is a day for some very serious reflection.

Prayer

Mary, my Mother, as the caretaker of my heart, I look to you to help me in responding to my Christian vocation. I offer my *yes*, but I need your motherly guidance to ensure that I am sincere and genuine in my response. Stay close to me these days, so that I will remain faithful to my calling, and act with responsibility for the privilege that is entrusted to me.

SECOND MONDAY OF ADVENT

I am every person in the gospel

To personalise and deepen my own involvement in the gospels, it helps if I consider that I am every person in every story. At times I can be the Prodigal Son, at times his self-righteous brother, and there are occasions when I can be the forgiving father, who can make friends with my shadow, and reconcile the wounded pride in me that lays loads of guilt on that part that has strayed off the straight and narrow. At times I can be the fussy Martha, at other times the reflective, contemplative, and listening Mary. I can be the wise men who look for signs, or the resigned and bored shepherds whose only company is sheep, and whose voice means little to anyone else. I may be like any of the Jewish people, waiting for my Messiah, for my lucky break, waiting for my boat to come in, without any great hope that things will ever change. There is no point in speaking about a Saviour to people who are not convinced that they need one! If, however, I am prepared to recognise my blindness, deafness, dumbness, leprosy, or demons, I will have every reason to get excited about Christmas. This is for me! The Light of the world is coming into my darkness. The Saviour is coming looking for the sinner, me. If I were the only person on this earth, Jesus would still have to come, because there is absolutely no other way that I could make my own way back to the Garden.

'Those who sat in darkness have seen a great light.' 'Man/woman will live forever more because of Christmas Day.' 'God loved the world so much that he sent his only

Son …' I could rephrase that to read, 'For God loved me so much that he sent his only Son.' While acknowledging that, no, I am not the only person in the world(!), I can still prepare my heart for Christmas in the sure and certain knowledge that Jesus does want to make his home there, to set up his kingdom there. OK, Jesus came to take away the sins of the world, but only those who acknowledge their sins, and open their hearts to his forgiveness and love, will really benefit directly from it. I am not saying, nor do I believe, that those who do not accept this offer of redemption will be excluded from the kingdom. There are millions of people on this earth who know nothing about Jesus, and who know of no reason why they should get to know him. I'll leave that one to God, absolutely sure that God's love and mercy will be offered to them in some other way. What I speak of here are those, like myself, and you, gentle reader, who have been told the good news; I believe we will be held responsible for how we did or did not respond to it. Jesus didn't go around healing anybody. He went around with the power to heal, and those who stopped him, and asked him, were healed. There were many lepers, blind, crippled, and diseased people who, for whatever reason, did not stop Jesus, did not call out to him, did not ask him, and they gained nothing from the fact that Jesus walked along their road. For the purpose of this reflection, I just want to stress that it can help me in my own preparation for Christmas if I become aware of my own need for healing, forgiveness, and freedom from bondage. When I die, I will not be asked whether my neighbour, my relative, or some chance acquaintance chose to take Jesus seriously. Neither am I excused from being concerned about their welfare and salvation. My greatest contribution to them is that I should open my own heart to the fullness of salvation, so that I might become a channel of his love to those around me. My responsibility is to give witness, whether others choose to follow my example or not. St. Francis said that we should always preach the gospel and, only when we have to, should we use words.

Action

Imagine the following scene: You are sitting on the roadside just outside of Jerusalem, and you see a crowd coming towards you. After some time, you notice that Jesus is right there in the middle of the crowd. This is your big moment. Would you make an effort to go towards him? He stops, comes over to you, looks at you with great love, and whispers, 'What do you want me to do for you?' What do you think your answer might be? Take some time out today, and, if helpful, jot down some words that come to mind. (No need for details, in case the paper blows out the window!). Try to make this situation as realistic as possible, because he will come into your house this Christmas, and he will ask you this very question. Remember that Jesus knows you through and through, so there's no point in waffling on, just for the sake of giving him an answer. This encounter can be as personal and as real as you want it to be.

Prayer

Jesus, Lord, I invite you very especially to make your home in my heart this Christmas. I pray that during this time of preparation your Spirit will enlighten me as to where I am most in need of your healing touch. I believe, Lord, help my unbelief. Lord, increase my faith. Lord, to whom else can I go? You, and you alone, have the words of eternal life.

SECOND TUESDAY OF ADVENT

If I were in Bethlehem

When I was a child, like St Paul I thought as a child. At Christmas time, I just could not understand how anybody could have turned Mary and Joseph away, when they came looking for lodgings. In my innocence, I was convinced that I certainly would have welcomed them in, and, indeed, have given them the best room in the house. My thinking has changed over the years. Life has taught me that some things just don't change. When I look at the situation now, through the eyes of the good people of Bethlehem at that time, I'm fairly sure that I would have made some excuse, or perhaps just closed the door, without any need to offer an excuse. There have been many times in my life when I have found myself in similar situations, with different people, in a different time-frame. I can be very selective whose cross I'll stand under. There are people who come to my door and, once I see them, they are immediately put into a particular catalogue. There are those who will be welcomed with a hug, and brought straight to the kitchen for a cuppa. If they have travelled, they may well be offered accommodation for the night. There are those who will be welcomed, and will receive whatever priestly ministration they sought, and escorted to the door again. There will be others who will be left outside the door, while I bring them out a cup of tea and some bread. Then there are others whom I will check out through the spy-hole of the front door, and the door may not be answered at all. I am not proud of this, but it's so easy to see Mary, Joseph, or Jesus in some people, as long as they are sober and don't smell and swear!

I cannot imagine Mary or Joseph being in any way repulsive or off-putting, but I could easily see how they could have been overlooked. They would have lacked the brash aggression that demands and gets attention. They were probably meek, timid, and quite intimidated so far from home, in a strange place. I honestly believe that, alas, I too would have let them go unnoticed, to attend to someone with a better chat-line.

So far, this has been me allowing my imagination run all over the place. However, thank God for Christmas! At least, I get another chance. Oh yes, I can be sure that I'll meet many people between now and Christmas who will look towards me for a helping hand, a kind and welcoming word, and a little human dignity. I may not have to leave my own house to find some of them. If Christmas is to mean anything, it must surely include hospitality. I personally know several families who always provide an extra chair or two at the Christmas table for those who have neither chair nor table of their own. Oh, I can meet and entertain Mary and Joseph without any doubt, if I choose to. If my heart is open to such kindness, I will certainly find them; and if it's not, I won't even notice them, even if they lived next-door. Christmas is a good time for stock-taking in the whole area of kindness, hospitality, and common decency. It is a time to make amends to God, and to repay his prodigal generosity to me by sharing some of his many gifts with those who do not have. I believe now, that, if I had lived in Bethlehem, with what I now know and believe, I might have made some effort, but, alas, hindsight often means no more than looking backwards.

Christmas gives us all many chances to get in touch with that better and more generous side of our natures. There is no reason that at least one of the 'breakthroughs' I make this Christmas in my treatment of others, may not continue into the coming year. After all, this is central to living Christianity, and not some extracurricular agenda added on to salve our consciences for a day or two. Christmas is a season for giving, and that is good. Spreading that giving to those who can give nothing in return, is a further step along that road of forgiveness.

Action

As these daily reflections continue, I have a feeling that the noose is closing in on me! Not really, so let's not panic! However, if we are to be sincere at all about Christmas, then our lovely generalities must become concretised into activity, and become realities. The test of our maturity is our willingness to mediate these generalities down into the specific. Give some thought today to someone in particular for whom you are going to go out of your way to befriend this Christmas. Some elderly person living alone? Someone bereaved over the past year, and this is the first Christmas without a beloved one. In this case, you have the luxury of choosing the Marys and Josephs you will entertain. In the events, there will be other opportunities where your goodwill can overflow, and spread the blessings of the season. Yes, we are given yet another chance to get it right. It certainly won't be God's fault if we still persist in getting it wrong.

Prayer

Mary, caretaker of my heart, please supervise the preparation of the manger of my heart. Obtain for me the gift of a generous heart. Please pray with me, in me, for me, that I may be open to the hospitality that you would wish me to show those others. Jesus told me that whatever I do for others, he will take as being done for him. I need you alongside me, to ensure that I avail of all such opportunities. You probably were the first person at Cana who saw that there was a problem; and you certainly were the only one there who knew what to do about it. I have so much to learn from you, in my relationship with, and my attitude towards Jesus. I look to you as my teacher, as the one who will guide my steps.

SECOND WEDNESDAY OF ADVENT

The Holy Land

I had the privilege of accompanying groups on pilgrimage to the Holy Land on nine different occasions. I have happy memories of those times, and the many good and wonderful people I met on each occasion. We used the opportunity as a retreat, as we visited the most significant places mentioned in the gospel stories. The gospels came alive for us and, on returning home, we could read or listen to the gospel with greater awareness and understanding. When we arrived back in Dublin airport, we had one last gathering, before dispersing. My introduction to such a gathering was something like this: 'Now you've been there, and seen many things for yourselves. I believe it should be the ambition of every Christian to visit the Holy Land at least once in a lifetime, even if this hope is never realised, just as all Muslims try to make a trip to Mecca at some time or other. There is no need to return. From now on the Holy Land is within the heart of each of us. From now on, Bethlehem, Nazareth, Calvary, and the Upper Room are to be within our own hearts. You can visit Bethlehem in your heart any day you choose.' I went on some more, but that is the general gist of what was said, before we went our separate ways.

In recent times, Bethlehem has been anything but a peaceful and tranquil place, and events there and in other places have made it increasingly more difficult to think of Israel as the Holy Land. This, however, should not be the case within our hearts. If I really want to get to know Jesus personally, and I desire that his message should come alive for me, then I must become familiar with the gospels. I can read the very same passage in a gospel very slowly several times. The first time is to discover what it is saying. The second time is to read it for my heart, so that I can get a feel for what it teaches, or what it shows me about Jesus, and how he interacted with others. On the third occasion, I can read it as if I were actually there among those gathered with Jesus. By moving along slowly, with several readings, I enter into the scene, and I begin to apply the situation directly to myself. Imagine doing that with the Bethlehem story. As I read it, it is like peeling back layers of wrappings, and getting into the core of the message. By doing this, I can end up on my knees at the manger. 'This is *now*, and I am *here*.' I spend as long as it takes absorbing the whole atmosphere, taking in each item in turn. I kneel with Mary, and allow her speak to me about what's happening, and *what* this has to do with me, and *why* this has to do with me. I listen to Joseph, and come to learn what he is thinking. I am there when the shepherds arrive, and I observe every moment of their time there. I am also there when the wise men arrive, and I hear their version of events. They explain their science, and how they were able to discern from the star that something unusual was afoot. I ask them to explain the reason for each particular gift they brought. Especially do I sit by the manger and reflect on this extraordinary miracle, a God in sheer powerlessness, in a place that was probably not even marked on a map.

Yes, this is my Bethlehem, this is my Holy land, and this is *now*. I depend totally, of course, on the Spirit of God within to reveal the wider implications of this scene that is unfolding before me. I learn how this is intended to effect my life directly.

Action

One of the loveliest moments on Christmas morning, is when parents bring their children forward to view the crib, and to kneel there. The Christmas presents have long been opened, and the waiting and wondering is over. Now it is time to bring them to the crib to reflect on the 'the reason for the season'. I believe it would be most helpful if we, adults, as part of our preparation for Christmas, went down into our hearts each day, and spent some quiet moments reflecting on what is happening there. As Christmas approached, I'm sure that Mary grew more and more conscious of the life within her, and she entered her heart to ponder on this wonderful miracle about to be unfolded. I don't believe she had any full idea of all that this involved, but she must certainly have known that this was very special indeed. Join her in quiet prayer today, and especially ask her to keep you very close to her during these days of preparation. Think of words like waiting, expecting, anticipating, preparing today. All around you, with each day, there are more and more external preparations going on for Christmas. Use this as a reminder to visit your heart, and reflect on the preparation, waiting, expectation, or anticipating that is going on there.

Prayer

Mary, my Mother, you can accompany me any time I wish, as I go to the sacred shrine of my heart. I can find my own Bethlehem there, but I depend totally on you to keep me close to you, and to make that time as life-giving and realistic as possible. For you, that first Christmas was an extraordinary personal experience. It was something that you had long awaited, and, even as you held the dead body of Jesus at the foot of the cross, you must have remembered the first time you held that body in your arms that first Christmas night. Please help me to personalise that Christmas event this time round, so that nothing that happens around me may come anywhere near the joy and celebration that I experience within my heart.

SECOND THURSDAY OF ADVENT

My chance

As we make our way along these *Stepping Stones to Bethlehem*, hopefully the reflections become more personal, more real, and more specified. I mentioned in an earlier reflection what I fancied myself as doing had I lived in Bethlehem all those many years ago. That is totally irrelevant now, because things are of such a nature that I can insert myself in the situation, and do now what I should have done then. It matters little what I *might* have done then. I am truly blessed to be given yet another chance. It is neither implied nor expected that there will come a time when I'm really going to get it right! We are not saints! Christmas is about 'peace on earth to those of goodwill'. This is a time for garnering all the goodwill at my disposal, and for opening my heart to *all* that God wishes to give me. For example, a simple approach to prayer would be something like this: I find a place and a time when I can be still, and free from immediate concerns. My prayers begins with the words 'OK, Lord, I'm here! I've shown up! Now you take over!' The important things to remember are that I show up, and that prayer is what the Spirit does after that. I can approach this Christmas with the exact same mentality. I will endeavour to have all the goodwill I can muster. I suspend my own hidden agendas, and prepared menus, and I leave it to the Lord to make the most of what I have to give.

Whatever I have is enough. At Cana, they only had water but, when this was made available to Jesus, he could do the needful, and supply the need. Later on, they had but a few loaves and fishes, but when these were placed at Jesus' disposal, nothing was the same again. 'Something beautiful, something good. All my confusion he understood. All I had to offer him was brokenness and strife, but he made something beautiful of my life.' I become very uncomfortable at Christmas-time with expensive gifts. I become afraid of an element of competition entering in, where one person feels obliged to return something even more expensive. Some of the most precious gifts I have received back along the years have been home-made by children. Christmas was long gone, and they still adorned my desk, because I could never bring myself to throw them out. (For years I had the centre of a toilet roll, colourfully decorated, set on a flat stone, and that was my pencil holder!) It is fashionable to complain about how commercial Christmas has become, and yet we all can get sucked into the hype and the rat-race, and all sensible and meaningful values go out the window. This particular Christmas is *my time to bond afresh with the Lord.* Nothing should be allowed get in the way of that extraordinary grace. Of course, I will buy presents and send cards to others, and Jesus would certainly want me to do this. On a personal level, however, this is a very special occasion, and it is something that I really want to celebrate. I am not thinking of, nor am I suggesting some sort of ego trip, of a me-and-God, and forget about the rest of you . Quite the opposite, in fact. I could be totally involved with choir, St. Vincent de Paul, and several charity dinners for the homeless. Apart from all that, however, I still must come down to my own personal *yes* to Jesus at Christmas. I cannot just presume that Jesus is somewhere in the crowd, if I am not personally aware and conscious of that fact. Even Mary and Joseph made that mistake. They were nearly home when they discovered he wasn't there at all! Yes, this is *my* Christmas in so far as I can only celebrate it when I join my *yes* to Jesus, to his *yes* to the Father. (I am also expected to do this at every Mass, as I place the drop of water in the chalice at the Offertory.)

Action

No matter how I present these reflections; no matter how inspiring or banal they may be; no matter how repetitious and abstract my suggestions may appear, *nothing whatever is going to happen if I don't take time out to pray.* It is only at a time of quiet prayer that these reflections will come to life for you. We are all very conscious of the amount of effort and money that is spent in the preparation for Christmas in most homes. It can happen that this Christmas is still going to bring bills in my front door for several months to come. I speak about prayer with even greater urgency and importance, while leaving the seriousness of your response entirely in your own hands. Even if I could, I would not attempt to write something that will make everything perfect and OK for you this Christmas. If you don't make your own personal input, then nothing is going to happen, no matter what books you read, or sermons you hear. Today must include some serious decisions about times and places for quiet prayer, if we are to make the most of the days ahead. I don't need to be any more specific for now, because we will be returning to this on several other occasions between now and Christmas day.

Prayer

Holy Spirit, Spirit and Breath of God, please guide my heart into 'Prayer Mode', and lead me into an openness to prayer today. You are living within my heart, and I ask you, please, to stir my heart into new life, and to generate a sincere desire and hunger for prayer there. Prayer may not come naturally or too spontaneously to me, and I will need that constant nudge, that frequent reminder. With all my heart, I say *yes* to your presence within me, depending totally on you to energise my spirit, and to inspire me.

SECOND FRIDAY OF ADVENT

Dispelling the Darkness

The world into which Jesus came was one of darkness and oppression. The country was under tyrannical oppression by a foreign country. Even in the God-area of religion, the people were very bound by repressive rules and regulations from a group of power-driven and self-righteous controllers. The wise men were guided to Bethlehem by the light of a star. The angels appeared to the shepherds as the whole sky was lit up. Jesus had come as the Light of the World. He had come to those who sat in darkness and in the shadow of death. 'Those who sat in darkness have seen a great light.' Satan was 'the Prince of this world', and hope was in short supply. The darkness prevented God's people from seeing a way out. There was little or no personal freedom, either politically or religiously. God was confined in the Holy of Holies, and this was definitely beyond the reach of any but those in compete control and authority. Candles feature largely in our celebration of Christmas. When I was growing up in the country, part of the Christmas tradition was to have a candle burning in the front window of every house, as a sign of welcome to the passing stranger. Even this has been 'hi-jacked' by the secular world, with the plethora of fairy lights and gaudy Christmas lights down the main street of every town.

Bringing this to a personal level, we all have areas of darkness within our own hearts and souls. This can come about in many ways. The person who is facing Christmas for the first time without the presence of a loved one who died during the year, must surely be aware that a bright light has been extinguished in the home or in the heart. Those who are away from home for the first time can experience a sense of being in exile, far from the flickering and welcoming light that comes from the fire in their front room at home. The greatest darkness of all, of course, is within the heart that does not experience love and belonging. This can begin at the human level, and it reaches its zenith with the absence of any sense of the warmth and light of God's love. Each one of us can experience this at different levels. Christmas presents us with an opportunity to invite Jesus to enter our hearts, and to dispel *all* darkness from there. Part of the preparation, in most parishes, is a Service of Reconciliation during the week coming up to Christmas. It's like rekindling the baptism candle, when we can begin again. Salvation is not something I receive after I die; it is the grace to start again today, or any day I choose, no matter how far down the road of darkness and despair I may have wandered. As my generation grew up we had religious exercises that, while good-intentioned, may have left many of us with some serious handicaps, when it comes to the openness which I consider to be necessary to reap the full benefit of Christmas. Take 'Confession' for example. Most of us had our weekly laundry list, and very little changed from week to week; and, worse still, nothing much was expected to change! We made most of the decisions, as we examined our consciences, lined up our sins in order of seriousness, species, and number, and this is what was handed to the Lord! (The Lord himself had very little say in it.) Imagine what might happen if Jesus was given permission to take over the whole process. He might well come up with a completely different list! He would see darkness in areas within our spirits of which we were totally unaware. He might probably point out sin where we considered there was virtue. The Pharisees were very religious people, and they made every effort to remain faithful to the law and the commandments. This, however, led to a form of religious intolerance and pride towards those less perfect than themselves. The story of the Pharisee and the publican is a case in point. The Pharisee told the Lord about all the wonderful things he did, and how better he was than the publican. This was blindness, indeed, and blindness is a very real experience of perpetual darkness. The publican, on the other hand, must have had a fair amount of light within, because he could clearly see that he was a sinner.

I suggest today's reflection on light and darkness, because it could provide us with a wonderful approach to all that Christmas represents. If I am open to the light of God, then I am open to Christmas. If the coming of Jesus into my heart dispels all lurking darkness there, then my Christmas will be blessed indeed. As a child, I used be afraid of the darkness, because it was inhabited with spooky and frightening creatures. Imagine the transformation within the human heart when the fullness of Jesus' coming is accepted there. The end result is that the heart, and indeed the person, becomes a very real and evident Christmas Light, which is part of the vocation of being a Christian. The spooky and the frightening creatures are dispelled from within my heart, and I would surely become aware of a sense of peace, and freedom from fear.

Action

It is said that you're as sick as your secrets. If there could be any recognisable good coming from the revelations of child abuse over the past few years, it must surely be that, at last, some of the victims have been given an opportunity to have their stories heard. Imagine spending a whole life with such horrors bottled up inside, never once being brought out into the open, because of the lack of compassion, understanding, and even simple belief. That must be horror indeed, and certainly is a very frightening form of darkness. I would suggest that each of us has our own closets, containing various hurts, resentments, and guilts, that we may never have faced up to. I am not suggesting any kind of therapy here, unless someone decides that this is necessary. What I do suggest, however, is that it is not being very realistic to invite Jesus to make his home in my heart, and to think that I can deny him access to the rooms and closets where my darkest secrets lie concealed and unrevealed. For today, it may be sufficient to do a little soul-searching, trying to imagine what Jesus would see, if he were allowed full access to my inner being. It may be sufficient to identify them now, and make a resolve to deal with them over the next week or so. If there is anything serious there, it won't require any length of time to locate it, and become aware of it. What to do about it will be very much part of the reflections of the following pages.

Prayer

I invite you, Spirit of God, to shine the light of your truth into every corner of my heart, and to reveal to me very clearly each and every area there where Jesus' coming must be free to change, to heal, and to free. Please give me the courage to name, claim, and tame my demons. Even if the prison doors are flung open, I cannot be dragged out into freedom; that has to be my decision. I give full access to every area within my whole being, and ask you, please, to shine the light of your truth into every nook and cranny.

SECOND SATURDAY OF ADVENT

Messiah

Throughout their history, the Jewish people had found themselves, again and again, in exile, or in bondage of one kind or another. There is no denying that they have always been a Chosen Race but, as Teresa of Avila, at a moment of pique, said to God one time, 'If this is how you treat your friends, it's no wonder you have so few!' In their darkest moments, they always lived with the hope that, one day, a Messiah would come to redeem and rescue them. 'Messiah' means 'the Anointed One' and, therefore, would be someone sent by God. Throughout the centuries the prophets kept this hope alive and, to this day, the Jewish people still await their Messiah. When Jesus came on earth, some of the Jews accepted him as the long-awaited Messiah, and it is from these that the whole Christian tradition grew. Not for one moment do I believe, or am I implying that those Jews who did not accept Jesus, have missed the boat, and will never be redeemed. I'll leave all of that to a kind and compassionate God who, of course, must still have a special plan for his Chosen People. For us, as Christians, though, we accept Jesus as our Messiah, and we look to him as the one who will lead us out of exile into the Promised Land. In him we find redemption, salvation, and forgiveness of sin. We look to him as the one who has removed the yoke of bondage, and who is fully committed to bringing us safely home. A point that must be made here, however, is that I am not automatically a Christian, just because I was baptised, or my family have been Christians for centuries. What makes me a Christian is my willingness to accept Jesus as my Saviour, as my Messiah, and I look to him as the one who will bring me back to the Garden. This declared willingness must come from my own heart, and cannot be superimposed on me by family, church, school, or society.

At the very core of my upcoming Christmas celebrations, must be a renewal of my personal acceptance of Jesus as my Messiah, as my Saviour. Just as married couples can, and ought, renew their marriage vows on a regular basis, so should I renew my commitment to Jesus, and my acceptance of his commitment to me. Christmas time is as good a time as any to do this, while acknowledging that anytime is a good time, as long as it happens. While not pretending to be a scripture scholar, I can allow myself the freedom to imagine that Jesus probably had to come into his own personal awareness of his mission. Any of us who have any experience of trying to walk in the ways of God become aware, as time goes on, that we have been called to fulfill a particular mission that is uniquely ours. Our creation wasn't something that happened at the whim of a whimsical God. I can easily accept the fact that Jesus grew into his awareness of the particular mission that was his. I also believe that the level of my commitment to Jesus can be at a deeper level each time it is renewed. That is why I should not let this special time pass without renewing my Christian commitment, and accepting Jesus, yet again, as my Messiah, as my personal Saviour. I cannot live today on a *yes* I said yesterday. We are familiar with the attitude expressed about 'Oh, no, not Christmas time again!', and all the negative reactions about Christmas becoming too commercial, and that we'll all be glad when it's over, etc. For the Christian, this particular Christmas has never happened before, and the opportunity it provides me for deepening my Christian commitment is completely new, and totally refreshing. There is no reason why I should get sucked into the honky-tonk jingle bells, even if all around me do so. The kingdom of Jesus will always have to compete with the kingdom of the world, and that will remain so until the end of time. If anything, the more the world attempts to hijack Christmas, the more determined it should make me in defining and clarifying where I stand. Right from the beginning of Christianity, many millions of Christians paid with their lives because of their decision to follow Jesus, and accept him as Messiah. I can look around at today's world with a certain amount of despondency and pessimism. I wonder when will all this terrorism end, and when will nations begin to come together in unity. Amidst all my despondency, the bottom line is, 'Lord, let there be peace on earth, and let it begin with *me*.' As I stand before God, that is my most important response, and in most cases, it often can be my only response.

Action

Do you have a baptismal cert.? I mean do you actually have one in your possession, or at least within reach? If you have, maybe you should remove it from its wraps for the rest of Advent, and carry on your person at all times. Make a photocopy, if you wish, and place a copy near the mirror in your bathroom. This may sound crazy, but I honestly don't apologise for suggesting *anything* that will contribute in any way to the deepening of my Christian growth and commitment. We can be horrified at suicide bombers choosing to bring havoc and destruction to others at the expense of their own lives. While I see nothing to commend such actions, I cannot but be amazed at the zeal and fanaticism that would drive young people to blow themselves to pieces for something they believe in. It would be different if there were Godfathers in the background, manipulating or ordering them into action. The evidence is, however, that there are more and more such zealots only too ready to die for something in which they believe with such a commitment. Surely it's not asking too much of me to, at least, be willing to acknowledge my Christianity, even through such a simple thing as carrying my baptism cert. on my person, or wearing a Christian symbol, not as an ornament, but as my own personal declaration of where I stand, and who I follow.

Prayer

Mary, my Mother, I often wonder when you yourself became aware that Jesus was the Anointed One who had been so long awaited by your Jewish nation. I look to you to help me in any attempt I make to fully accept him, and to open my heart to the fullness of all the redemption and salvation he came to bring. My prayer to you is that this Christmas might be more than just a memorial of something from the past, or even a celebration of all that it signified. I sincerely want to personalise this sacred season, and I look to you as the one who will accompany me every step of the way. Thank you for being with me at this time.

THIRD SUNDAY OF ADVENT

Faith

Faith is a response to love. Don't ask me to trust anybody until you have first convinced me that the person loves me, or has my welfare at heart. How often, in the gospels, do we see examples of encounters with Jesus which illustrate this point so very well. By word of mouth, or through physical evidence, someone came to the conclusion that Jesus was a good man, who really cared for people. For whatever reason, that was their conclusion, and that was a primary factor in them acting as they did, whether it was in asking for a healing, or simply touching the hem of his garment. The second factor, of course, was a simple conviction that, of themselves, they were powerless to do anything about their condition or situation. These two basic facts combined to create a miracle. 'I can't; he can; so I'll ask him.' My reason for choosing this theme for a reflection today is because Christmas is about just how much God cares for us. 'For God loved the world so much that he sent his only Son …' Taking this as the core expression behind Christmas, it is only logical, then, that my response to all of that should be so vital. Once again, I say that faith is a response to love.

To grow in faith, and to build up my faith, it is necessary that I grow in my awareness of God's love for me. This love is very clearly expressed through the whole revelation of Christmas. God could have decided to love us from a distance, but he decided to come down to where we're at, to become one with us, even to the point of kneeling at our feet in humble service, as he washes our feet. Coming as a helpless child might not be our way of planning such a momentous event. We would have organised Committees, and International Organisations, based on multi-coloured ethnicity, and financed by large corporate donations. We would have had a Welcoming Committee, a Public Relations Committee, etc., etc. I use the etcs., dear reader, to spare you all the details! While all this would be going on, a little child would have arrived on this earth in some back-of-beyond place that none of our planners had ever heard of. That's just how God does things. His love is total, it is unconditional, and it is offered with graciousness. All that God asks in return is that we believe his offer to be real, to be true, and that we respond to his generosity with acceptance, gratitude, and love. When I speak of God expecting our gratitude, I do not mean that God is building up some sort of fan club, that will proclaim to the world how wonderful he is. When we appreciate God's love, we come to trust him more, and we allow him do for us, in us, and through us all that is within his will for us. *The only limits to what God does for us, in us, and through us are the ones we ourselves set.*

I speak of faith as a virtue here, not as one of the gifts of the Spirit, something better suited to a reflection for Pentecost. When I speak of the virtue, I speak of something that I can practise, something that I can grow with, and become better and better at doing, to put it as simply as I can. If I exercise my faith in small things, it will be so much easier to exercise it in greater things. Faith is something in which I can grow every single day. My response to God's love this Christmas should be so much deeper than it was last year. Therefore, my openness to celebrating and appreciating this wonderful time should be so much more exciting. I have come across people who become more depressed with each new Christmas. They are confused between Christmas as celebrated in the world, and Christmas as celebrated within the human heart. In a real way, I can have the best of both worlds. It would be wrong to cut myself off from the world's celebration of Christmas, and to absent myself from the family celebrations, and the gatherings of the clan. I can take part in the cards, the Christmas tree, and the holly, while being deeply aware what the real celebration is all about. In fact, I might suggest that, it is only by taking part in the holly, jingle-bells, and mistletoe parts that I can witness to what my own reason for celebration is all about. The kingdom of Jesus is *in* the world, even if it is not *of* this world. It is within this world that I am asked to live out my Christmas vocation, and it is in the marketplace that I am asked to give my Christian witness.

Action

How about sitting down for a while, and having a chat about love. I mean, what do you say it is? How do you know when you're loved? More importantly, can you point to a specific time in your life, and feel sure that God was showing his love to you at that time? Remember the comment above: The only limitations of what God does in our lives are the ones we set. It would be wonderful if, today, through some honest soul-searching, you came to realise just how small your God really is. The smaller your God, the bigger your problems. Mary magnified the Lord. How could you do that? You have to, you know, or your problems will be really magnified. The word 'love' is the most abused word in any language today. It often has nothing to do with acceptance, compassion, or belonging. It may not necessarily include forgiveness, which is the only thing that will keep love alive. I honestly think that I would be at a great disadvantage if I approached Christmas without any clear idea of what *love* is all about.

Prayer

Mary, my Mother, please let me join with you in praising and magnifying the Lord. Expand my heart to receive more and more of his love. Lead me along the road of faith as I prepare to celebrate this wonderful day of God's love. Your love for Jesus was very special and very personal. You are a Mother who shows her children what love is through her love for them. Please teach me the true nature of love, and cultivate this within my heart. I would so much want to meet God's love with my love this Christmas, despite the infinite gap between the two. I know, as you knew, that God's love extends across every divide, and fills up every chasm. Please keep me very very close to you, as I try to open myself to love that is so far beyond any ability of mine to comprehend.

THIRD MONDAY OF ADVENT

Hope

The only real sin I can commit, as a Christian, is not to have hope. In yesterday's reflection I spoke of faith as a response to love. Now I speak of hope as something that I *must* have, if the real meaning of Christmas is to come alive within my heart. Jesus enters the darkness of our despair to dispel the clouds, and to let the light of his love enlighten our hearts. Once again, he takes that whip of cords, and he rids the temple of my heart of the negativities, the guilt, and the discouragement that often accompany the human condition. Hope is something that involves the future. I cannot see down the road ahead, but it is hope that prompts me to venture. In a way, it is but another expression of faith and, indeed, a very definite declaration of my conviction about God's love for me. When Jesus came on earth, he brought hope to a people who saw no way ahead, and who believed that things would always be as they were. When Jesus called Peter, we are told that 'He looked at Peter.' Later on, when Peter denied him, Jesus once again, 'Looked at Peter.' Peter saw that the look had not changed, and there was a way back for him. No wonder he wrote in his second letter: 'Always have an explanation to give to those who ask you the reason for the hope that you have.' Judas, on the other hand, saw no way out, and he just threw in the towel, and gave up.

'Hope' is defined as 'to cherish a desire for something, with some expectation of obtaining it; to look forward to a good with a measure of confidence'. Hope includes expectation, confidence, and anticipation. It is something very positive, and not just hanging in there by my finger-nails, terrified that the branch might break. For the Christian, hope is something very special. Hope needs to be highlighted at a time like Christmas, when we celebrate a hope that was restored to a world exiled from God, with no way home. Hope dispels and liberates, and it gives excitement to the heart. There is a great need for hope in today's world. This has always been the case but, because of communication, we are more aware of the areas of death and despair that are so evident in so many places across the globe. Without wishing to generalise, I think it is reasonable to assume that the prevalence of depressions of various kinds, and the increase in the suicide rate, can be directly connected to the absence of hope. I think it is also reasonable to make a connection between this situation and the growing materialism and secularisation in our world. 'Put Christ back in Xmas' is a cry that we hear every year. I would suggest that Christ is as much at the heart of Christmas as he ever was, while our awareness of that, and our interest in that has become quite blurred indeed. That is why I consider it so necessary to approach each Christmas as if it were the very first one. Salvation is the grace we get to start again. Advent is a time of preparation, a time out, when we can slow down, reflect on what it's all about, and approach the occasion with a whole new resolve. It is so easy for us to drift, and how often do we discover that Christmas, Easter, summer holidays are upon us, without us being aware. At this stage, I feel that I need to move on to the 'Action' section, because, by nature of the subject, I consider it calls for action more than reflection.

Action

It is said that the incoming tide raises all the boats. Find a time and a place today where you can be as free from distraction or interference as is possible. Imagine a fountain of living water rising up from within your heart. A spring has been released somewhere in the core of your being, and the water continues to rise, bringing all the wreckage and baggage of life to the surface with it. Without you being aware of that, quite a lot of wreckage of life has been dumped down this shaft over the years, and it was like a leaden weight that always prevented you from 'take off' out of the quick-sands of your own selfishness. Very appropriately, the Greek word for conversion is 'kinosis', which means to empty out. This rising water within is a process of conversion, of emptying out, so that the water can overflow, and you can become an oasis in the desert, to which others can come to be refreshed. Can you identify anything in particular among the wreckage? In particular, can you identify areas of despair, situations and realities that you may have accepted were always going to be there? Can you identify something that you had just given up on, and never expected to change, to remove, or to improve? Take as much time as you possibly can on this, because you are on the threshold of a whole new freedom here. To settle for something is a denial of the fact that God can do all things, can change all things, can make all things new again.

Prayer

Holy Spirit, Breath of God, you are that fountain of Living Water that is to be found at the very core of our beings. Focus your torch of truth on those areas of darkness within my soul that must be named, claimed, and tamed, if I am to be healed, and to open my heart completely to the extraordinary outpouring of God's love this Christmas. Dispel from my heart all demons of despair, and, as part of this season of new life, awaken within me a whole new hope, based on the power and reliability of God's promises.

THIRD TUESDAY OF ADVENT

Love

How can I speak about Christmas without highlighting the story of love of which it is such a unique expression? Yes, Christmas is the world's greatest love story. 'God loved the world so much … God loves each one of us so much …' That is the story of Christmas. Even in the not-so-Christian celebration of Christmas, love is seen as central to the season. It is a time of gift-giving, of being in touch with friends, and the coming-together of families. It is significant that most people attend church services at Christmas, even if many of them don't darken the door of the church until the following Christmas. A particular effort is made to raise money for charity in the weeks leading up to Christmas and, on the day itself, there are special centres set up to ensure that even the homeless are provided with a Christmas dinner. Generally, Christmas brings out the best in people, and many express the forlorn wish that Christmas might last a bit longer within the home.

Love, by definition, is to accept another actually as that person is, and to be willing to help that person move from there when ready. God loves me exactly as I am, but he loves me more than that, or he would leave me as I am. Love is to accompany another, and it always includes compassion, or the ability and willingness to share the pain of another. By coming among us, Jesus was clearly showing the Father's love in a practical, evident, and tangible way. He would prove this all the way to Calvary, and say 'Greater love than this no one has, than that a person should lay down a life for a friend.' If this Christmas is to be a season of love in my life, I can think of no better way than to open my heart to the love that is being offered me. The more love I receive the more I have to give, and the more love I give, the more I receive. 'Where there's no love, put love, and then you will find love' is a saying attributed to St Iraneus. There is one very important fact that I should refer to much oftener in these reflections, or indeed in everything I say, write, or do. It is exclusively the work of the Spirit to open my heart to God's love, and to reveal that love to me. Otherwise it remains just a lovely idea, or a general theory, that in reality has very little meaning or effect. This is something to which I should deliberately advert on a regular basis. It is just not possible for the human mind, of itself, to have any hope of being able to comprehend the width, height, depth, or general extent of God's love for us. 'Flesh and blood has not revealed this to you' were the words of Jesus to Peter. Jesus also tells us that no one knows the Father except the Son, and those to whom the Son chooses to reveal him. Kneeling before the crib on Christmas morning can be a moment of quiet revelation. I bring my need to be loved to that place, and I open my heart to be filled with the love of God. Mother Teresa said that the greatest hunger on earth is not for food, but for love and belonging. 'Come to me all you who labour, and are heavily burdened, and I will give you rest ... and you will find rest for your souls,' is the call of the infant from the crib. Lay down your burden by the crib, and drink from that fountain of life and love. Come here to be refreshed.

Action

Most of us will admit to things within ourselves that we don't like. This may be real, or it may be imagined, but the imaginary is very real to the person who imagines it. Asking Jesus to love those things in me that I myself don't like, does not mean that this will automatically include his approval or approbation. There are things there that need to be removed, whether it be a resentment, an addiction, or a pattern of destructive behaviour. I still can bring all of these to Jesus, and ask him to separate the wheat from the chaff. There is an Arabian proverb which says 'A friend is someone to whom one can pour out all the contents of one's heart, grain and chaff together, knowing that loving hands will sift it, keep what is worth keeping and, with the breath of love, will blow the chaff away.' I would suggest that today you would make a particular effort to pour out your heart to Jesus, in the hope and expectation that he might love what is worth loving, and blow the rest away. Make this a day in which your heart is open to the coming Christmas, with a conscious desire to personally experience the love that it implies. Imagine yourself pouring out your heart, grain and wheat together. What do you identify as grain? What do you identify as chaff? You are being asked today if you are really willing to accept Jesus as your personal friend, someone who can change everything.

Prayer

Heavenly Father, thank you for the gift of your love that is poured out on us through the coming of your Son Jesus. Through the action of your Spirit, may my heart be fully open to receive a real outpouring of that love, so that I may genuinely celebrate this Season of Love with a sincere heart. I have tried to fill the emptiness inside in so many ways, but without success. I now have found the fountain of living water, and I ask you to make my heart an oasis in the desert. Make me a life-giving person for those whom I meet on the road of life.

THIRD WEDNESDAY OF ADVENT

Promises

My generation grew up on promises. I made promises on a constant basis – New Year's Day, Ash Wednesday, etc. At this stage of my life, I wouldn't have to be a rocket scientist to realise that my track-record in the promises stakes has not been too good! Christmas is God fulfilling his promise. He had promised to send a Messiah, and he did. Jesus is the fulfilment of the hopes of all the prophets down the ages. I'm sure there were many times when the people despaired of that promise ever being fulfilled, and I can empathise with the Jews of today who are still awaiting the arrival of their Messiah. God is always faithful to his promises, and Jesus himself declared that heaven and earth would pass away before his promises would pass away. He gave his word, and he keeps his word. No wonder Jesus is often referred to as the Word of God. This Word (or promise) of God became incarnate among us in Jesus Christ. My response to Christmas is one of gratitude to God for doing what he promised he would do. When I have fully accepted the promise that Christmas contains, then, and only then, can I be in a position to make any promises in return.

What did God promise? He promised that he would send Someone who would deliver them from all bondage incurred through original sin, Someone who would lead them back to the Garden. Jesus tells about a farmer who sowed good wheat in a field. After a while, the servants came to him, and asked him, 'Was that not good wheat you sowed?' When the man says that it was, they ask about the weeds that have now appeared. 'Where did they come from?' 'An enemy has done this', they were told. (The word 'Satan' means 'enemy'.) When the servants asked if they should remove the weeds, they were told to leave them there, and the farmer himself would take care of them, 'Lest, in pulling up the weeds, you pull up the wheat as well.' This story is about us. When God created us, he saw that we were good. After original sin, the weeds of sin, sickness, and death appeared, which were not, of course, part of God's creation. Rather than have us attempt to rectify the situation, and end up doing more harm than good, God said that he would take care of the situation himself. It was to remove these weeds of sin, sickness, and death that Jesus came. God's promise was fulfilled when Jesus came to remove those weeds, and to restore our original innocence.

An important part of our preparation for Christmas is to become more and more aware of our need for redemption, our need to be freed from the corruption and pollution of sin, sickness, and death. There is not much point in speaking about a Saviour to someone who is not convinced that he is a sinner. Jesus said that the Spirit would convict us of sin, and lead us into all truth, which is basically to say the same thing. For God's promise to me to be fulfilled, I must accept it, and benefit from it. When the sinner comes to accept the freedom from bondage, that sacred promise is complete, and God's promise has been fully realised. I said earlier that my generation grew up on promises. I must be growing in wisdom in my old age (!), because I have ceased to make promises, and to give as much attention as I can to the promises Jesus makes to me. 'The sin of this world is unbelief in me' he says, and this must surely include a refusal to believe his promises. Elizabeth said to Mary, 'All these things happened to you, because you believed that the promises of the Lord would be fulfilled.'

Action

When I speak about sin, I am not thinking of particular acts; rather am I speaking about the human condition, and the attitudes that we inherit because of our damaged nature. One generous act doesn't prove that John is a generous man. (He could be a candidate in the next local elections!) Similarly, one sin doesn't mean that Carol is a sinner. No, Carol is a sinner by nature, just as if I went to live at the North Pole I would still be an Irishman. When I speak of sickness, I am not thinking of fevers, diseases, hospitals, etc.; rather am I thinking of a certain malaise within our nature that is less than healthy or life-giving. We can have several forms of emotional or moral sicknesses that would never show up on an X-ray. There are three questions that I suggest you should ask yourself today. How do I experience my sinfulness, and how aware am I of some sort of basic rebelliousness deep within my psyche? Can I identify something in myself that is not life-giving, whether that be fear, anxiety, guilt, poor self-image, self-condemnation, etc.? How do I feel about the thought that my death is drawing nearer with each day? All of these must be brought to the Lord, who came to remove these very same weeds. There is a clear and definite promise made to you, which you can choose to accept or reject. You could also take a serious look at whether you believe the promises of the Lord at all. Like me, are you still someone who is preoccupied with your promises to God, and may not take his promises too seriously. Plenty of room for reflection here.

Prayer

Lord Jesus, sacred Promise of the Father, I accept you as my personal Saviour and Redeemer. I ask you, please, to take over in the wheat-field of my heart, and to remove the weeds of original sin that are there. Through your death and resurrection, you have set us free; you are the Saviour of the world. With all my heart, Lord Jesus, I want you to be Lord, God, and Saviour within me, and I want to belong totally to you. You give yourself totally to me this Christmas, and I, such as I am, offer you everything that I am, and everything I possess.

THIRD THURSDAY OF ADVENT

Patience

God is infinitely patient. His acceptance is always held out to me, whether I accept it or not. No matter how many Christmases I have been on this earth, his offer is just as new and as fresh today as it ever was. Time, of course, as far as life and this earth is concerned, will run out and, for each of us, the sands of time continue to flow along relentlessly. This often lulls us into a smug complacency, until something like a heart attack, or a malignant tumour wakens us from our slumber. I won't always read the death columns in the morning papers. One day, my name will appear there, and I won't be around to see my name in print! I remember, some years ago, visiting an elderly lady in a nursing home. She was a good friend, had a wicked sense of humour, and I never had to choose my words when I spoke to her. It was New Year's Day. As I wished her a Happy New Year, she remarked, 'Yes, indeed, Father, another New Year is upon us.' I smiled and replied, 'Yes, Annie, you're beginning another spin in the washing-machine of the Lord but, in your case, I'd say it'll be the final rinse!' She laughed heartily, and told everybody that came along what I had said. When I did her funeral just before Easter of that 'final rinse', I couldn't help thinking just how frail our earthly existence is, and how little we are in control of it. I must confess that it didn't bring about any great con-version of heart about the precious nature of time, or the urgency of the present moment. There is, however, a very serious side to the present moment, and this coming Christmas might be more timely than I could imagine. I do not believe that fear motivates too well, but perhaps a little dose of realism might be of some benefit. One thing I do know: This Christmas is a gift, a once-off gift and, no matter how long I live, this particular gift will never be repeated. In choosing themes for reflection over these days, I cannot say exactly why I should have chosen patience, beyond the fact that God continues to repeat his offers, and he continues to invite us to his banquet, year after year, after year.

Surely God has a right to have some expectations from us, even if he doesn't demand anything. Unrequited love tends to run into the sand. The offer is made to us, and God is prepared to wait again and again, in the hope that, eventually, we take him up on his offer. One thing I am grateful for is that the offer is not a once-off, or we would all be in trouble. Christmas does speak of 'peace on earth to people of goodwill'. With my own personal experience of human nature, I don't think in terms of complete and instant conversions. Rather do I envisage a gradual process, a slow but sure yielding on my part to the love and longings of my heavenly Father. Surrender is a gradual process, because of our nature. It is as if I surrender, town by town, village by village, just as we have witnessed in the recent conflict in Iraq. The invading forces had hoped for, or expected a quick and total surrender within a few days, and were surprised at the level of resistance they encountered. It is something the same with us, except we are not under attack from God, even if we are bombarded with invitations to surrender. Christmas is a time for cards, and one of those is always from God, with RSVP written all over it! When I speak of God's patience, I do so, thinking of who would ever continue to send me invitations if I had refused to reply to the previous fifty or sixty! God is not like us, however, and, Christmas after Christmas, until the time I die, I will continue to receive this personal invitation to surrender to his love, to accept the offer of divinity from someone who has come to share in our humanity. 'Long have I waited for your coming.' I can imagine the father of the prodigal son scanning the horizons every single day, and eventually his hopes, prayers, and patience were rewarded. There is a Russian legend about the Day of Judgement. The people are flocking in the gates of heaven, and Jesus is standing at the gate. He has his hands held up, shading his eyes from the sun, as he peers off into the distance. Someone asks him what he is doing, and he answers, 'I'm waiting for Judas.'

Action

This is a day to think about surrender. Religion tends to be about control, while spirituality is about surrender. Religion is external, and it is what we do, while spirituality is internal, and is about what God does in us. This is a day to reflect on conversion from religion to spirituality, like Paul on his way to Damascus. Paul himself tells us that he was one of the most religious people of his day, as he zealously followed all the rules and regulations of his religion. He then goes on to describe what happened, which led to the scales falling from his eyes, and his new vision of a God of Love, rather than a God of Law. This is something we could all reflect on today, as we prepare to kneel before the crib. It is significant that the large outer gate of the basilica in Bethlehem is closed, and one enters through a small entrance, where each person has to stoop, and climb through, as it were. There is something here about making myself a bit smaller, if I am to enter this sacred spot. Yet another example of the camel and the eye of the needle. (Incidentally, what Jesus meant, when he spoke of the eye of a needle, was one such narrow entrance at the side of the Temple, which was known by that name.) I speak of surrender, because this is a fitting response to the patience of the Lord's love. If this Christmas includes a conversion from Religion (Law) to Spirituality (Love), then it will be a truly blessed time indeed.

Prayer

Mary, my Mother, I turn to you for this one, because you must have been so aware of the constant love, and extraordinary patience of God. Your humility was such a powerful force in your willingness to surrender to God's will in all things. Please help me prepare my heart for this Christmas time. I can see in God's love for me what Paul means when he says that love is patient. I do want to respond to that love, and I need your guiding hand to get me moving along that road of response.

THIRD FRIDAY OF ADVENT

Longing

I begin this reflection by asking myself why I chose the word 'longing', above every other possible word, as a title. The only reason that comes to mind is that I am very much aware of a hunger or longing within the human spirit, that God most certainly does acknowledge and answer at Christmas. He does this all the time, of course, but this is clearly emphasised in our Christmas celebrations. There is a hole in the human heart, and we can try to fill that in any way we choose, but it can be filled by God, and only with God. 'You have made us for yourself, O Lord, and our hearts can never be at peace until they rest in you,' to quote St Augustine. The road of life is strewn with the human wreckage of those who have tried to fill this void through substance abuse, pleasure, wealth, power, and many other ways. The results have always been the same. One dictator after another have fallen, and left it all behind. If wealth brought happiness, then why should a millionaire commit suicide? If health brought happiness, then why should so many young people, with all of life before them, decide to throw in their cards, and give up? Nature detests a vacuum, and will always try to fill it. It is into this vacuum that I place Christmas, and everything it stands for, in this reflection. On that first Christmas night, there was no room in the inn. Many a home, and many a heart have been closed every Christmas since then. This is my opportunity to make available every bit of emptiness inside and invite

Jesus to make his home there, and to 'fill my house onto the fullest'.

I remember a nativity play some years ago, being presented by young adults with mental disabilities. One young lad had but one line; he was to tell Mary and Joseph that there was no room in the inn. All went well until his big moment arrived. Mary and Joseph knocked on the door, and he came out. They asked if he had any place where they could spend the night. He looked at them, and then he looked back at the space behind him on the stage, and he told them to come on in! I know it was really funny on the night, but I have often thought of the profound message behind that simple gesture. We all have plenty of room. We have time to pray, if we decide to take time out to pray. We have time to visit friends, those in hospital, those recently bereaved, etc. I am not talking about working myself into a frenzy, and having no time just to flop and relax. Becoming a Christian does make a difference to how I spend my time and my money, but it is much more than that. Each one of us has a genuine longing for God in our lives, whenever we take time out to become aware of that. The average person walking down the road believes in God alright, but they're not fully convinced that they need him right now. Sometimes it takes an emergency, when we look for God's phone number under our emergency phone numbers, to wake us out of our slumber. God is always on standby, only too eager to join us in the fray.

Imagine the following scenario: I gather a group of people around me, each chosen for some particular reason. Each has become aware of a restlessness within, and they seem to miss real peace by inches. I speak to them. I tell them about God, and his plan for us. I tell them how God's promises are realised in Christmas, and I invite them to try God's way this time round. We gather around the crib. I share a reflection on what all of this represents. I pray with them and, through use of their creative imagination, I bring them to a personal encounter with this new-born baby. This baby is looking for some place to lay his head, some heart to call his home. He brings with him the fullness of God's power, disguised in the weakest of human beings, a newly-born child.

Action

I deliberately cut short the reflection, because you, gentle reader, are the one I bring to that crib today. You do have some real longings in your heart. You have thirsts that have never been quenched, hungers that have never been satisfied. At the end of it all, you sometimes felt that there just had to be something else. This is your day to acknowledge this. Jesus speaks of those who hunger and thirst for justice. There are so many who hunger and thirst for love. It is important that I stress the starting point here, or I'll set out with a shopping list which God is expected to supply! It is in Jesus and in Jesus alone that my longings will be fulfilled. It is right here, coming up to Christmas that those longings should be acknowledged and declared. All of these reflections for Advent, hopefully, will help us lay down markers of areas that need attention, of hurts that need healing, of hungers that need to be satisfied. Above all, they should highlight the longings in the heart of God, who longs so much to pitch his tent among us, and to make his home within us. Once again, we are dealing with a moment of *truth* here. Adam and Eve fell for the lie in the garden, and they came under new management, as it were. We are led out of that darkness by a Spirit of Truth and, inch by inch, bit by bit, area by area, we are brought to face those things in us which must be redeemed and rescued from bondage of every kind. As God longs more and more for more and more of our inner selves, so that he can really fill us with his Spirit, we ourselves also have a similar desire for the very same thing, whether we recognise it as readily or not. Christmas is a wonderful meeting place for God's will, and for those of goodwill.

Prayer

Spirit and Breath of God, please stir up within me a zeal and enthusiasm for things of God. Enkindle within me the fires of divine love, so that I may have a genuine and sincere longing within my heart for all the wonderful blessings that are made possible throughout this Christmas season. In my most honest moments I can be quite aware of the real longings of my heart, even if I dare not articulate them, even in prayer. I accept this Christmas as a moment of grace, just like blind Bartimeus was told that 'Jesus of Nazareth is passing by'. I don't want to miss this wonderful opportunity for grace and blessing. I ask you, please, to open my heart fully, so that the fullness of God's love might be poured out upon me. With all my heart, like Bartimeus, I cry out to the Lord, because I am open to his full attention, and I want to present myself to him with all my blindness, and everything else within me that is in need of his healing touch.

THIRD SATURDAY OF ADVENT

Yes

Jesus said that we were either for him, or against him, and he asked that our 'yes' be 'yes' and our 'no' be 'no'. Make up your mind, in other words. In Creation, God said a very definite *yes* to us, to our existence, and to our welfare. Original sin was us saying *no* to God. We would do things our way, and we refused to obey. Jesus was God's final and eternal *yes* to us, and he became, for us, the new and eternal covenant. Jesus was very insistent that he and the Father were one. They who see him, see the Father; those who hear him, hear the Father; and those who obey him, obey the Father. He never said anything unless the Father told him, because all his life was also a total *yes* to the Father. He came to fulfill his Father's will in everything and, through his obedience, he would become the antidote for the disobedience of humankind. Jesus went on to tell us that, as the Father sent him, so he was sending us, and our obedience to him would be our evidence that we love him. He laid great store on our response, because all he could do was *offer*, and nothing happened until we *accepted.* Our *yes* of now wipes out for all eternity every *no* we ever said or lived. As we approach yet another Christmas, it is vital that we do so with sincerity, and with a willingness to co-operate fully in God's plans for our good. When we speak about Jesus in the Mass, we use the past tense: 'Dying, you destroyed our death; rising you restored our life. By your cross and resurrection, you have set us free.' His part of the covenant is completed, and now it's over to us. Jesus has come among us, and everything depends on whether we accept him or not.

The hard facts show that both Jesus and his message have made relatively little impact on the world as a whole. Enormous good has flowed from that fact, of course, and the on-going potential for goodness is infinite. The harvest is great, and the labourers are few. God is patient, however, and his New Covenant continues to be held out to all who are willing to accept, and this will continue to be the case until the end of time. For the sake of this reflection, however, I must narrow down the focus to Christmas, as it effects us as Christians. The very name 'Christian' implies a decision to follow Christ, and to live out his message in the world. Our Christmas hymns include a line which says 'Man will live for evermore because of Christmas Day'. Yes, for the Christian, Christmas is a time to rejoice, to celebrate, and to renew our commitment to Jesus. It is a time to live through the whole wonderful good news of salvation all over again. When the Jews celebrate the Passover, they read the whole story once again from the Torah, of how God delivered them from slavery in Egypt, and brought them into the Promised Land, and they renew their commitment to the Covenant that God made with his people. When Muslims celebrate Ramadan, all of the Koran is chanted over the loudspeakers of the mosques for a full month, while the listeners gather to respond to the call of the Prophet. I could have used the word *response* instead of *yes* as a title for this reflection. The reason I chose *yes* is that I am only too aware that *no* is also a response. Christmas is a time for Christians to rally around the crib, and once again to give thanks to God for this wonderful expression of his love. I mentioned in an earlier reflection that the highest numbers of attendance at church are recorded on Christmas eve and Christmas night, and this is good. These are people who are saying their own *yes*, even if they choose not to repeat it in that way during the rest of the year. It shows that such people haven't changed their *yes* of the previous year, and are still on line with what Christmas is all about. It is not possible for any of us to measure the depth of another person's *yes*, and it would be very wrong for us to pass judgement in any way on those who show up in church once a year. I have no doubt whatever that Jesus is delighted to see them.

Action

It is a great privilege to be able to say *yes* to Jesus. Many of us have grown up on what I might call the 'spirituality of addition', when our expression of religion consisted of more and more prayers, as if we were building our own Tower of Babel, and were building our own stairway to heaven. I have the privilege of celebrating Eucharist each day with elderly folk in a Retirement Home, and I often have to deal with their worries and concerns about no longer being able to maintain the same level of praying. This causes concern, and presents its own level of guilt. I try to help by explaining what I choose to call the 'spirituality of subtraction', when our prayers become less and less, and end up with just one word: *yes*. Mary began with that word, and many of these lovely and good folk arrived there aged ninety. Mary said *yes*, and the Spirit did everything else. Mary didn't actually *do* anything, but she gave God permission to do whatever he chose to do with her, and through her. This Christmas is a time for my own personal *yes* to Jesus, and to everything he stands for. How, when, and where I should say that *yes* is up to me, but it is important that it be a well thought-out *yes*, and something that comes from my heart. Try and let your *yes* be as central to your thinking today as possible.

Prayer

Mary, my Mother, please join with me in saying my *yes* to Jesus this Christmas. Help me to be sincere in saying it, and to be fully aware of its implications. I invite you, please, to accompany me in a special way during the week ahead. I have no reason to trust myself at all. Sometimes I say *yes* with total sincerity, and I crash at the first hurdle. I know that, of myself, I do not have what it takes to be consistent and entirely faithful to my word. This is where I look to you, to take my hand, and guide my steps along the road of fidelity, generosity, and courage. I believe that, with you by my side, I can say my *yes* with a reasonable expectation of being able to live it. Thank you.

FOURTH SUNDAY OF ADVENT

Manger

When I was a child, I laid great stress on the abject poverty of the stable, the manger, and the swaddling clothes (whatever they were!). I believed that I was growing up in a palace by comparison. The big consolation I felt for the poor wee baby Jesus was that he had a cow and a donkey breathing hot air on him! (No, we did not have central heating, so that evened the stakes a little.) No matter how the biblical scholars continue to reinterpret the events of those times, and to explode many of my childish mental images, I still hold on to the idea of the manger. It matters little whether is was a manger or a feeding trough. I am living in today, and the 'manger' today is nowhere else but in my heart. From the point of view of welcome, comfort, and warmth, indeed, it may not be so much better, but that need not be so. 'Something beautiful, something good; all my confusion he understood. All I had to offer him was brokenness and strife, and he made something beautiful of my life.' The first thing about my heart is that it be open, and that I am willing that Jesus should make his home there. The second thing is that I am willing that he effect whatever changes he chooses to make there, so that he can set up his kingdom there, and that his Spirit can flow from there to those around me, either through the words I say, the prayers I pray, the life I live, or the very person that I am. Unlike the wise men, or the shepherds, I don't have to travel to Bethlehem anymore, because Bethlehem is within my heart. Oh, yes, I will still visit the crib, and will view each item there. I will recall all those events of long long ago. However, when I get up from the crib, I won't be leaving anything behind me. I will be taking it all away in my heart. A few years ago, I heard a First Communion group of children singing a song, 'Oooh-ooh-ooh-ooh-ooh, heaven is in my heart …', and I thought just how appropriate that song was for them. As I walk away from the crib this Christmas, I too could sing that song.

This is a prayer that I like to say after Communion, and I offer it here in the hope that it might be helpful as we think of Jesus making his home in our hearts: 'Thank you, Jesus, for coming to me. I ask you to make your home in my heart, to feel at home there, and to be at home there. Please set up your kingdom there. Put all the enemies there under your feet. Proclaim your victory within my heart, and hoist your flag of victory there. Take your whip of cords, and rid the temple of my heart of everything that is not of you. Thank you, Lord, for coming to me.' When I receive Communion, I open my heart as well as my mouth, to receive Jesus. I want him to make his home at the very core of my being. It is there that my demons live, and it is there that he must enter, if he is to rid the temple. On the surface, I could be quite 'religious', and not show any evidence of inner anxieties, jealousies, resentments, or destructive elements of any kind. Deep down at the core of my being, however, the real conflicts take place. I can live on such a superficial level of spirituality that Jesus is treated like a visitor, as it were, and he never gets past the front parlour! The kitchen sink is still full of the breakfast dishes, and the beds are not made yet! I want him to remain exactly where he is, until I (?!) get everything in order, and then

I'll bring him on a conducted tour of the house, when he can congratulate me on the good order and tidiness of everything. It may sound ridiculous, but I'm afraid this can often be the case. The sad thing about this is that Jesus came to clean out those very rooms. When he entered the house of Jairus, he was brought straightaway to the room where the little girl lay dead. No beating about the bush here; it was obvious where the problem was, and there was no attempt to disguise it. That's all Jesus asks of us when he comes to us this Christmas. Imagine a circle, with Jesus at the centre. You are at the edge, and you want to come close to him. Your problem is that there are things in your life getting in the way of your coming to Jesus, sins, patterns of behaviour, weaknesses, etc. If you could get rid of those first, you would then arrive at where Jesus is, bloodied but unbowed, and he would pin a medal on you, and say 'Well done!' I know this sounds ridiculous, but it is something that can happen. The ideal thing to do, of course, is to go straight to Jesus exactly as you are and, with him, you then take on each sin and weakness one after the other.

Action

Take some time out today to reflect on what I have written about treating Jesus as a visitor who is kept waiting in the front parlour. OK, so your heart may not be the warmest place on earth, but it's to your heart that he wants to come. When he saw Zaccheus up on the sycamore tree, he called out to him, 'Come down, because today I want to dwell in your house.' Jesus has chosen to make his home in your heart, with your permission, and this Christmas time is a wonderful occasion to take this idea seriously. Hold on to this idea today, and experience a real desire that this might be so in reality. Jesus is our Saviour, and he just loves saving us, and freeing us from bondages of every kind. If you get a chance today, reflect on that circle I spoke about. What are the things that you see as coming between you and Jesus? Try to follow my advice, even for a short while, knowing that you can return to this on many occasions in the future.

Prayer

Mary, my Mother, caretaker of my heart, this is where I really need you! Jesus has chosen my heart as his home this Christmas, and I don't feel either ready or worthy. Please take over, and prepare the manger of my heart. Help me to open out my heart, and to be as willing as I possibly can to allow him have full access to every room in my house. You were the purest and most perfect human being that God ever created, and yet you felt totally inadequate at the thought that God should make his home within you. You can imagine then how I feel! I look to you to make up for all that I lack. What a difference that would make! That would even make me confident, because now I know there would be love, welcome, sincerity, and genuineness, things that I myself might not have in any great abundance.

DECEMBER 20

Peace

'Peace on earth to those of goodwill' (Lk 2:14). That is the promise of Christmas. This peace is special, because it is the peace of Jesus, which is not the peace the world gives (Jn 14:27). No earthly power can bring peace. All the UN or NATO can do is stop or prevent a war, but peace is not the absence of war. When my heart becomes the manger, then that is where the peace will come. 'I am leaving you with a gift, peace of mind and heart' (Jn 14:27). It is important to remember that this is pure gift, not something that can be earned or merited in any way. It is a question of Jesus sharing his own peace with us. Peace is what we experience when our relationships are the way they ought to be. It is not a question of getting all my relationships in right order, and then I will receive this gift. I would suggest that both actions run parallel to each other. As I am working at getting my relationships in right order, I will experience more and more peace, and will thus be enabled to complete the task. Part of my preparation for Christmas is to become a peacemaker in any way I can. 'God blesses those who work for peace, for they will be called children of God' (Mt 5:9). I can make use of this season of goodwill to mend fences and repair broken bridges between myself and others.

Remember it was Jesus who first spoke of peace. He is the one who offers it, and so we should be ready to accept the gift. This time of Christmas is a wonderful opportunity to open my heart fully to the peace of

Christ. This may well include celebrating the Sacrament of Peace or Reconciliation. In the whole area of my relationships, I sometimes find that I'm not getting on too well with God, myself, or someone else. Christmas is an opportunity to make amends, to set things right. A Christmas card, a phone call, or a personal visit to someone who has become estranged from me, could prove a wonderful source of inner peace. It matters not that my gesture be requited. All that matters is that I myself am prepared to make the effort. 'Whatever house you enter, first bless them, saying "Peace to this house". If a peaceful person lives there, the peace shall rest upon him. But if not, the blessing will return to you' (Lk 10:5-6). Christmas is a time for gift-giving, and peace is one of the most beautiful gifts I can give another. If I have peace in my heart, then that is transmitted through everything I do, and every word I say. Quite a number of our Christmas carols speak of peace on earth, and goodwill among people. As we approach Christmas itself, it is time to prepare my heart for this wonderful gift of God. Because Jesus offers it, I can be sure to receive it, if I am willing to. To have a yearning and longing for peace must surely be an inspiration of the Spirit. If that longing is there, then I can be sure that God would never put it there if he were not prepared to fulfill it.

Jesus came to reconcile us with the Father, and to bring us back to the Garden. He wants to lead us back from exile, which was occasioned by original sin. This reconciliation brings peace, and this is something very definite and tangible. If our hearts are open to the gift, we will experience that peace. There is no greater way to celebrate Christmas than to have peace of mind and heart. Christmas is a time for home-coming, for reconciliation with God, myself, and with others. The gift of peace brings us back in line with the heart and will of God. Without being open to, and receiving this gift, we cannot possibility celebrate this wonderful occasion. Jesus represents the Father's hand being reached out in love and friendship to us, and it is a gift that must be accepted with gratitude, humility, and sincerity. When I fall on my knees before the crib I declare my willingness to accept this most precious of gifts, a peace that only Jesus can bestow.

Action

If you can, take time out right now, open your heart, and ask the Spirit to pour the peace of Jesus into your heart. Repeat this prayer again and again today. If an opportunity arises, go aside on your own for a while. Use your creative imagination. Become deeply aware of your breathing. As you breathe in, imagine that you are breathing in the peace of Jesus. As you breathe out, imagine that you are breathing out all tensions, anxieties, and fears that may beset you. Continue with this as long as possible, until you become deeply conscious and aware of his peace within your spirit. Ask Mary, as caretaker of your heart, to supervise that peace. Ask her to be a peacekeeper within your heart, so Satan will not be able to come and steal your peace.

Prayer

Lord Jesus, I open my heart to you, and to your peace. In a very special way, this Christmas, I want you to make your home, to feel at home, and to be at home in my heart. Please pour out your peace into my heart, and let it displace all fears, anxieties, or worries that may lurk there. Let there be peace on earth, and let it begin with me.

DECEMBER 21

Mary

One of the surest and safest ways to enter into the heart of the Christmas season is to ask Mary to lead me, and to prepare my heart. She was there at the birth of Jesus, and she would also be there at his death. Her heart was the first Bethlehem, even before Jesus was born. She was the only person who could hold up the body of Christ, as at the Consecration, and say 'This is my body'. It was she who was chosen to give flesh and blood to the Word of God. In the words of the poet, she is 'human nature's solitary boast'. It is almost impossible to exaggerate the centrality of her role in the whole story of incarnation. It's not so much a question of anything she herself did; rather it is about what she allowed God to do in, with, and through her. She is our perfect model, if we are to touch, or be touched by this great event that we are about to celebrate.

The most wonderful thing for us, of course, is that her role only begins at Bethlehem. Because of that event, and as a result of it, each one of us is entrusted to her as our Mother, who will continue to bring us to birth as Christians, and who will guide us along the Christian way towards the fullness of the kingdom. At the very moment when Satan thought he had thwarted God's plan in the Garden, he was warned that a woman would crush his head, and he would lie in wait for her heel. Mary is everything that Satan is not. She had an extraordinary humility, and was never in any doubt that the whole story of Creation and Redemption was the work of God alone, and anything that happened to her, and through her, was entirely and totally the work of God. 'He that is mighty has done great things for me, and holy is his name.' She magnified the Lord, which, in simple English, means she continued to make God greater and greater while, at the same time, she considered herself as less and less. It was this extraordinary humility that enabled her have such profound faith in the promises of God. She was deeply aware that the power was never hers, and when she wanted help at Cana, she went straight to Jesus with the problem. It is through her that I can learn how to approach this Christmas season. She is not the centre of Christianity, but she can be found right at the centre, and she leads to the centre. She points to Jesus, and asks us to do whatever he tells us. Jesus obeyed the Father in all things and, in turn, he told us that if we love him, we will obey him. Mary was totally obedient to God in everything, and she represents the complete opposite of Eve, who refused to obey.

When I speak of Mary, I speak more about a relationship than any form of devotion. She is my Mother, and she loves each of us as much as she ever loved Jesus. The shepherds and the wise men went to Bethlehem to meet Jesus, and Mary was there to welcome them. Elizabeth rejoiced when Mary visited her, because she brought the Messiah with her. Simeon was happy to die because he held the Anointed One in his arms, but it was Mary who made this possible. She was there on Calvary, when all the others ran away, and she was entrusted with the very precious responsibility of preparing the apostles for the coming of the Spirit, and the founding of the church. In preparing my heart for Christmas, I can think of no better way than to draw closer to Mary, and ask her to take over that preparation.

Jesus said he would not leave us orphans, so he offered us his Father, and he offered us his mother. He said this wouldn't work, though, unless we became like children. In our lives, it's only the body that gets older. The person inside is still a child, and always will be; still needing reassurance, and still whistling passing the grave-yard! To get in touch with that Inner Child is a wonder-ful help in securing my relationship with Mary. My earthly mother gave me a body, but, like her, that too will die. My Heavenly Mother is entrusted with that Inner Child, and that Child will never die. That Child is invited to become a real living member within the family of God for all eternity. In that family, Mary will continue to be my Mother. (It could be quite complicated if my earthly mother were still my mother, and then there's her moth-er, and her mother before that, etc., etc. And then, of course, there'll be those with no children … and the scene becomes more and more complicated!) No, I believe, even though I expect to recognise my earthly mother, that we will all be united with one mind and one heart, and all of our love, prayer, and praise will be directed in the one direction, to God, the source of every-thing that is good.

Action

To begin with, check what place Mary holds in your Christian life. I am not thinking in terms of rosaries, novenas, or pilgrimages. I am anxious to go to the very heart of the issue, and search for clear evidence that she is trusted, and is entrusted with the safety of my journey along the Christian way. She did in a perfect way all I am trying to do, and called to do as a Christian. What I want you to check on is your attitude, not your actions. Can you remember that first day you went to school, or the first time you went to a dentist? Was your mother with you? Would you have gone without her? Did her presence with you make a difference? Make a definite decision today to involve Mary in your life each day this week. I will be suggesting a prayer, but this is one that you could continue to say for what is left of Advent. I'm sure it's not necessary to say so, but I feel that I should stress the importance of praying from your heart to her; ask her with sincere confidence. Consider her accompaniment as something that will make this Christmas truly unique and blessed indeed. Her mission is not complete until the last of her children has entered heaven. St Padre Pio said that he would stand at the gates of heaven until the last of his spiritual children had entered in. Jesus gave us himself in Eucharist the night before he died and, with his dying breath, he gave us his Mother. St John tells us that he fully accepted her and, in turn, he became her second son, just as her first was dying. She is always a Mother, and she has a mother's heart. Nothing would please her more than that I should fully accept her, and have a sound and solid relationship with her, rather than some sort of pietistic devotion to her. We have all witnessed strong bonds between a son and his mother, or his father, that grew stronger with the years. That's what Mary longs for from us.

Prayer

Mary, my Mother, I ask you to take complete control of my heart this week. Be the caretaker, the housekeeper there, because I look to your love and care that my heart be as ready as is possible to celebrate this wonderful occasion. I can approach Christmas with excitement and expectation, if I know that you are in charge of the preparations. Thank you. One of the great blessings of this Christmas is that I can renew my commitment and relationship with you. Maybe I never told my earthly mother too often that I loved her. If she is now passed on, maybe I regret that I took her so for granted. I can catch up on all those loose strings now, through you, because, in you, I have a second chance to be a grateful and generous son. I want everything that you want for me this Christmas. As a child my earthly mother used ask me what I wanted from Santa. Well, for this Christmas, Mother, I want everything from God that you see that I need. Thank you for being there.

DECEMBER 22

Gift

Christmas is a time for gift-giving. Some people complain that this dimension of Christmas has got completely out of control. I won't comment on this because, in this season of goodwill, I will try to live and let live. Just because others act in a certain way doesn't mean that I have to, so there is not much point in getting all worked up about what other people should, or should not do. The point I wish to stress in this reflection is that, when it comes to God's love for us, we speak of *pure free gift* all the way. When I buy a gift for someone at any time, one of the things I make sure of is that the price tag is removed, before the gift is wrapped. There are no price tags on God's gifts to us. This applies just as definitely when it comes to God's greatest gift of all, the gift of his Son, Jesus, at Christmas, a gift that continues to be offered to us every moment of every day for the rest of the year, until the moment of death. It is absolutely pure free gift, given with unconditional love, and not demanding anything in return. Any response on our part must also be completely free, and not brought about by coercion or compulsion of any kind. That is why our response is so important, because my response is one that only I can give, and one that I freely and deliberately decide to give. God gives me the gift, and he waits for my response, whether it comes or not. From early childhood, the spirit of gratitude was instilled in us, and the rudiments of good manners were repeated again and again.

Love always looks for a return in kind, only because this evokes even a further outpouring of love. When we accept God's love, we then have love to share with others and, by doing this, we are opening our hearts to more and more of his love. It is for our sakes that God wants to continue to pour out his love upon us. 'Having given us Christ Jesus', says Paul, 'will the Father not surely give us everything else?' Christmas is such an extraordinary gift, and yet God wants to continue to pour out more and more of his love upon us.

In yesterday's reflection, I spoke about Mary's profound humility. Another way of thinking of this is to say that she was totally empty of self, and so God could fill her with his grace, and the angel could speak of her as 'full of grace'. Carol Houselander speaks of Mary as 'the reed of God', as an empty chalice, as an empty bird's nest. All of this is an attempt to illustrate that, like a reed, which is hollow, beautiful music can be produced by the breath of God; or an empty chalice, or bird's nest, which can be filled with the blood of Christ, or the possibility of new life within the newly laid eggs. On the other hand, we sometimes hear it said of someone being 'full of himself'. There is not much room in such a person for any love save love of self. The only limits to the outpouring of God's love and gifts in my heart are the ones I myself set. The Greek word for conversion is 'kinosis', which means 'to empty out'. We are invited to stand under the Niagara of the Father's love this season. This is not a once-off gift; rather is it an on-going gift, something that continues, like a fountain, to rise up within our hearts. This gift is for life, not just for today. The gift of Jesus contains everything I could ever need for all time, and for all eternity.

Action

Do I have a heart that is empty enough, open enough, and hungry enough to be filled with the fullness of God's love? Do I have enough realistic grasp of the facts (Humility?) that I am prepared to accept with sincere and profound gratitude the greatest gift that God can give a human soul? Is my heart filled with sincere gratitude, and reverent awe at the thought that God, in Jesus, should choose to make his home within my heart? 'Lord, I am not worthy …' Find a few quiet moments today to sit still, let the muddy waters settle, and become conscious of a deep inner hunger to be filled with God's goodness and love. Do you let the thought of your own unworthiness get in the way of your openness to the extraordinary nature of the gift? If you do, it shows that you still believe that there just has to be a price tag somewhere! Are you humble enough to accept the offer, whether you're good enough or not? This is a day for some very serious reflection, and a time when you begin to experience both a sense of excitement and urgency. St John writes in his first letter, 'Perfect love drives out all fear. If we are afraid, it is for fear of what God might do to us. And if we are afraid of what God might do to us, it shows that we're not yet fully convinced that he really loves us.' Faith has been defined as 'having the courage to accept God's acceptance'. At the moment of death, you will stand before God, with the canvas of your life opened wide … out to the every edges … nothing hidden any more … no excuses, cover-up, pretences, any more. How do you think you'll feel, and how does your present acceptance of God's acceptance help you when you think of that final encounter?

Prayer

Heavenly Father, thank you, thank you, for your love, and for the prodigal and generous love you pour out upon us at Christmas. Oh, Father, with all my heart, I want to receive this pure free gift with an open and grateful heart. In Jesus' name, I ask you, please, to pour out your Spirit upon me, so that the soil of my heart may be fully prepared to receive the fullness of your Word. I have no doubt whatever about your side of the Covenant, but I have no reason to trust myself. I depend on your Spirit to evoke a proper response within my heart. I am truly grateful, Father, and I sincerely and genuinely want to experience the reality of your love this Christmas. I trust that, in offering it, you will also make it possible for me to receive it, and experience it. Thank you.

DECEMBER 23

Change

Imagine the following scene. A group of people are gathered in a hall. Jesus walks in and begins to speak to them. He tells them most of what he says in the gospels. There is bound to be a response. That response will not necessarily be totally positive. It is possible that some may walk out in the middle of his talk. Others may grumble, and mutter under their breaths to those around them. Others may be waiting on him to finish, to ask questions, to seek clarifications, or to argue some point. It is possible that many may be completely and profoundly moved by what he said, while others are mildly interested. One thing is sure: Once Jesus enters into a group, you can be sure that his presence will cause division! Of course, I'm not saying that it is Jesus who caused the division; far from it. It's what he says that divides people, because some want to hear, and others can get quite upset about what he says. Jesus comes to comfort the afflicted, but he also comes to afflict the comfortable.

If we were alright as we are, Jesus would not have come, because this would not be necessary. 'Oh happy fault, that merited so great a Redeemer!' St Augustine says. Jesus comes as Saviour, because we are sinners in need of salvation. His coming is an invitation to us to change direction in our lives. Once again, I say that if we were headed in the right direction, there would be no need for change. I'm sure God saw that the Hebrews would never have found the Promised Land, if he had not send Moses to lead them there. As it was, Moses had a fulltime job to keep them on the move, and to direct them towards their destination. On several occasions, for example, when they worshipped the golden calf, a god of their own making, they were determined to do things their way. God called them a stubborn nation, that found it difficult to obey, and to be lead. Our reality is that, of ourselves, we just do not have what it takes to work out our own salvation. Because of original sin, the enemy is within, and there is a basic deep-rooted stubbornness and rebelliousness within our human nature. Christmas is a call to change. Jesus came as a helpless child, and he would later point to children as having the necessary qualities to enter his kingdom. Our condition was such that the Creator would have to re-create. I am sitting in front of a computer as I write. If this computer 'collapses', there is no way that I would or could attempt to fix it. I would bring it straight away to where I bought it, and expect those who put it together in the first place, to put it right again. As we approach Christmas we have Services of Reconciliation, and any sincere or serious preparation for Christmas must, of course, include an openness to change anything within that is in conflict with the message of love being offered. If I do not admit to this need for change, then my celebration will be very hollow indeed. My kneeling before the crib must include some sense of surrender. That is the greatest welcoming gift I could offer this Child. There is an extraordinary power in littleness. Herod was a man with great power, and he was very much in control, and yet this helpless Child scared and alarmed him! Surrendering to Jesus means stepping down a step or two out of my ivory tower, and coming to kneel before a little child. I saw a childless young couple some months ago, who had just adopted a baby girl from an orphanage in Bulgaria. That little angel had them on their knees with delight, with gratitude, with love. She was old enough to walk, and her father was rolling around the floor playing games with her. In other words, he had totally surrendered to her love, and she had captured his heart. That is part of Christmas, as I kneel before the crib. 'This is the day that the Lord has made.' 'If today you hear his voice, harden not your hearts.' 'Today is the day of salvation ...' Any response I make that does not include a genuine desire to open my heart to forgiveness, and the grace to change, would be very hollow indeed. At this stage, I feel that I should move onto the *Action* section, because my response must be practical, and not just some pious thoughts, and religious reflections.

Action

Jesus called himself the Way, the Truth, and the Life. He called his Spirit the Spirit of Truth, and he told us that only the truth would set us free. He cannot set us free if we are not prepared to face up to the truth. I am not thinking of any great or lengthy examination of conscience. I believe that if there is something in my life that is a direct contradiction to what is signified by kneeling at the crib, then that must get my immediate attention. I am not thinking of my sinful state, which is part of being human. I am thinking of an attitude, a relationship, a pattern of behaviour, or some specific conduct that flies in the face of God's love, and that I will not surrender, while still expecting God to give approval to that by turning a blind eye, and being implicated in my wrongdoing. We all have a conscience, that still inner voice that confronts us with our wrong-doing. That is the voice of God, a voice that must be heard, and responded to. 'Come back to me with all your heart. Don't let fear keep us apart.' Go to Confession, or attend a Service of Reconciliation if you choose to. More important than that, however, is a deliberate and conscious decision to return to the path of the Lord if, in some specific area, I have wandered down a road that leads me away from God. This is decision-time, and it is a golden opportunity for such decisions. Everything that Christmas represents is on the line here. Repent while there is still time, and let a Child lead you back into the arms of a loving and forgiving Father.

Prayer

Holy Spirit, Spirit of Truth, I ask you, please, to point out anything in me that is contrary to the will of my Father, and to the love that is offered me these days. Please help me believe that, with the call to change and to repent, comes the grace to respond to that call. Christmas is a time of goodwill. Please strengthen my will to take what-ever action needs to be taken, so that my heart can be filled with the fullness of God's love and forgiveness this Christmas. Jesus said that you would convict us of sin, and that you would lead us into all truth. I depend on you to do this, because I am only too aware that part of my sinfulness is my inability to see the truth. Jesus also said that you would reveal to us all about him, and would remind us of everything he had told us. I need that very much now, so that I can come to him with a heart that is open to forgiveness, to change, and to redemption from bondages of every kind. Please lead me to the truth, which is Jesus, and that truth will set me free, and I will be free indeed.

DECEMBER 24

Shepherds and Wise Men

I said in a reflection at the beginning of Advent that the gospel is now, and that I am every person in the gospel. The shepherds and the wise men represent two extremes of humanity. It is interesting that shepherds were considered as being totally unreliable when it came to telling the truth. If you spend enough time out in the open, under the burning sun, and sleep in caves throughout the darkest hours of night, there's no telling what sounds you might hear, or what weird sights you might see! We use an expression 'Tell it to the marines', when we hear something we absolutely refuse to believe, because sailors have also been classified as being among those with wild and weird stories of all that happened to them, and all the wonders they have seen. It's a kind of like the fisherman telling about 'the one that got away'. And yet it was to shepherds that the message of Christmas was first revealed. In fairness to them, however, they made a very wise decision. Being told a message by angels is fairly good authority, but they decided to go to Bethlehem and 'see this thing for ourselves'. This journey of the shepherds is one that every Christian must travel. We were told the message by parents, teachers, preachers, etc., but at the end of the day we too must come to find all of this out for ourselves. I can spend most of my life believing something just because my parents told me. There comes a time, however, when I must take responsibility for my own faith, because I cannot go on living with the faith of someone else. How can I come and see for myself? I discover that God answers prayers only through my own praying. I know when I am forgiven, and I can come to experience God's presence through becoming aware of it, in reflection and prayer. I learned to walk by walking, and to talk by talking, not by reading a book about it, or listening to lectures. It is the same with the message of Jesus. Until it becomes personalised for me within my own heart, through my own experience, it is not mine, and it cannot become part of my life. In other words, without this personal experience, and the conviction that comes from such experience, I cannot claim to live the Christian life.

Until the message becomes alive in me, there is no way that I can pass it on to others. The gospel is in between two sentences. The first is 'Come and see', and the last is 'Go and tell'. I cannot go and tell if I have never come and seen. The apostles were sent as witnesses to Christ's resurrection. This was possible only because they themselves had met him, spoken to him, listened to him, and eaten with him after his resurrection. They spoke of something they saw and heard. That is at the core of evangelising.

The wise men came from another spectrum of humanity. They were searchers, people who always had their antennae at full stretch, picking up all that was going on around them. They obviously believed that they had so much more to learn, and that they were surrounded by wonders and truths not yet revealed. There was a certain humility about them which, combined with a genuine thirst for the truth, motivated them to go to great lengths in search of the truth. They must have been honest and trusting men, prepared to make an effort to make their dreams come true. They watched for signs, and they must have had a deep awareness of something greater than themselves 'out there somewhere'. Such people always find God, in whatever way God chooses to reveal himself to them. They saw a star that was different from any star they had ever seen before. It meant something to them, although exactly what, they could not be sure. The star began to move, so they decided to follow. The star gave them a sense of direction in their lives, and it gave their lives a purpose. It is not necessary to reflect on all the possibilities of their journey but, yes, it brought them to Bethlehem. More wonderful still, they were humble enough to accept a new-born baby as someone very special, without being able to grasp the significance of that uniqueness. The final line of the account is very significant. Once they had met Jesus, they decided not to return to Herod, but 'they returned home on a different road'. What a wonderful symbolism for the Christian who, having found Jesus, owes nothing anymore to the Herods of this world. The Christian is one who travels home a different way from people of the world. They are free from following the crowd, and they now can set their feet on the road less travelled.

This Christmas can be an opportunity for me to approach the crib either with the heart of a shepherd who seeks confirmation of something I already have known; or I can approach it as someone who is already open and ready for new and greater revelations and discovery. The only gift I need bring is my goodwill and an open heart. I can be assured of a welcome, and I can experience a sense of home-coming. Even outside of Christmas-time this encounter can always take place, and I can continue to be assured of the same great welcome. The important thing is that I have journeyed from the simple stories of childhood, or the dreams of a star-gazer, and I have found the pearl of great price. Later on in the gospel story we are told that, after Andrew met Jesus, he ran looking for his brother Peter, and exclaimed, 'We have found the Messiah.' To proclaim this is the vocation of the Christian.

Action

Looking back at your life, can you identify steps of growth along the way to how you now perceive Jesus, as against your view of him in your childhood? Can you pinpoint particular convictions you now hold about him, and his message, that you have come to through your own personal experience? It is possible, you know, for a person to continue on a First Communion level of spirituality. I heard of a man who still confessed, at 85 years of age, that he hadn't done what his parents told him! They were dead for fifty years, but he never changed his shopping list since his First Confession. I had an uncle who said a prayer every night against having a toothache, and he hadn't a tooth of his own for years! Hebrews tells us, 'Let us leave the elementary teaching about Jesus, and move forward to a more advanced knowledge, without laying again the foundation ... God willing, let us move on now to other things.' Peter speaks in one of his letters about those who remain 'baby Christians', and who are still fed on milk, instead of solid and staple food. The big question facing you today, amidst all the holly, jingle-bells, and Christmas trees and lights: *What, in reality, does Christmas mean to me?* Nobody else can answer that question for you. Only you know the answer, and you will find it in your heart.

Prayer

Father, I thank you for the gift of your Son. I open my heart to welcome him, and I pray that his coming might redeem and rescue me, so that I might return with him to spend my eternity singing your praises. When I think of the shepherds and the wise men, I feel so grateful that, after all these years, I also am given a chance to go to Bethlehem to see for myself, or to bring gifts, and to worship. I am also grateful that, because of meeting Jesus, I can now travel a different way back home to you. He is my Good Shepherd and while I keep close to him, I know that I will always be safe. I would dread having to struggle along without any sense of direction, destination, or accompaniment. Thank you, Father, Creator, God, you have thought of everything, in your great love for us.

CHRISTMAS DAY

Welcome!

The blessings of this wonderful day on you, gentle reader, who have accompanied me throughout the previous few weeks. Jesus is here, and so are we, and the sinners have met the Saviour. The whole purpose of Christmas is being fulfilled as you read. 'Man/woman shall live for evermore because of Christmas Day.' It is usually easy to experience a sense of joy and goodwill on this day, but today is very special indeed. We welcome the gifts and give thanks for them. We give our gifts, and we try to mean what we say when we wish others the joys of the season. Above all, though, there is a joy of heart, mind, and spirit, that only the committed and sincere Christian can experience on this day. Jesus is the reason for the season! This is his birthday, and there are more candles lit today than during any day of the year. Even in the midst of World Wars, hostilities were suspended on Christmas day. The phone lines are jammed, and the churches are full. The streets are empty, and the kitchen table is laden. The lights flick on and off, and there is an air of festivity all around. And all of this even in a world which knows little and bothers less about Jesus. We don't have to regret that fact, however, because this, in a special way, is *our* Christmas. We don't begrudge others their Christless celebrations because, who knows, maybe something of what he said, or something of what he is, might seep through into the hearts of those who are searching. In our western world, it would be well-nigh impossible to live through this day without hearing some reference to Jesus, either through the crowds returning from church, the carol singers, or something on the television. If Jesus waited for everybody to welcome him, he wouldn't have come yet! It is a good day, a great day, a day where we celebrate, with as much love as we can with all of God's people, great and small.

Bringing as much generosity, goodwill, and love to the dinner table could be one of my most important prayers of this day. Some families invite a homeless person, or an elderly person living alone, to join them at the table. The telephone rings from family members in far-away places, all anxious to experience a sense of belonging on this very special day. We all get a glimpse of how things could be, and many of us experience what we wish life could and should be like. This is not a fantasy, however, and the very fact that we experience what we do must encourage us in our endeavours to make other days like this one. We are only too well aware that Christmas day is not a happy day for many people, because of circumstances in their homes or in their lives. We can experience a powerlessness to help, but the very fact that we would love to help if we could is, in itself, a good. And that brings me straight into our Action.

Action

I switched to this section abruptly, because I felt a very real desire that each of us should do *something* for those who do not enjoy what we enjoy today. Because these people are so far-flung, and so many of them are unseen and anonymous, I think it is absolutely essential that I fall on my knees for a minute or two today. Firstly, I give sincere thanks to God for his blessings to me and my family. I then ask him, with a sincere heart, that he send a blessing, a helping hand, a morsel of food, a tangible love to those who are most alone, isolated, marginalised, and forgotten on this Christmas day. I pray from my heart that my love and concern for them might be transmitted to them in some way, because nothing is impossible for God. If my family say Grace before meals, I should include these people, so that others around the table might add their prayers to mine. Without wishing to make decisions at such a moment, that I may find impossible to fulfill later on, I could, however, make at least one small resolve about some particular charity that will receive my help, however small, during the coming year. It is not possible for me to be grateful and to be unhappy at the same time. The greatest thanks I could give for what I myself have, is to wish to share that in some way with those who have not. If I can do this, I will have *arrived* at the very core of what Christmas is all about. And now, gentle reader, go and enjoy your Christmas dinner, and may this be a day of many and wonderful blessings for you and yours.

Prayer

Loving Lord Jesus, a Word of Love spoken to us by the Father, I welcome you, and thank you from my heart for coming to bring us safely home. I know there are many homes and hearts open to you today, and I am truly glad for that. I wish that everyone was ready to welcome you, but you understand, and I leave all of that to you. I can only offer you what is mine. It's not much, but it's all I have. I offer you all the love, goodwill, genuine longings, sincere desires, and deepest hopes that I have. I accept you with open arms, because I know that, when I have *you* I have everything. *Wow!* Thanks, Jesus. I won't debate about whether I'm good enough or not, or how best I should return your love, and all those things that pre-occupy my head, and bring me away from my heart. I pray for the humility to accept a pure free with no price-tag gift, without question, and with a very special *Thank you, thank you, Jesus*. Oh, and by the way, Happy Birthday!